80
Godey's
Full-Color Fashion Plates
1838–1880

Edited and with an Introduction by
JoAnne Olian
Curator Emeritus, Costume Collection
Museum of the City of New York

DOVER PUBLICATIONS, INC.
Mineola, New York

Copyright

Copyright © 1998 by Dover Publications, Inc.
All rights reserved under Pan American and International Copyright Conventions.

Published in Canada by General Publishing Company, Ltd., 30 Lesmill Road, Don Mills, Toronto, Ontario.
Published in the United Kingdom by Constable and Company, Ltd., 3 The Lanchesters, 162–164 Fulham Palace Road, London W6 9ER.

Bibliographical Note

80 Godey's Full-Color Fashion Plates: 1838–1880 is a new work, first published by Dover Publications, Inc., in 1998.

Library of Congress Cataloging-in-Publication Data

80 Godey's full-color fashion plates, 1838–1880 / edited and with an introduction by JoAnne Olian.
    p.   cm.
  ISBN 0-486-40222-3 (pbk.)
    1. Dressmaking—United States. 2. Costume—United States—History—19th century. I. Olian, JoAnne. II. Godey's magazine. III. Title: Eighty Godey's full-color fashion plates, 1838–1880. IV. Title: Godey's full-color fashion plates, 1838–1880.
TT520.A12 1998
746.9'2'097309034—dc21   98-44232
                                                           CIP

Manufactured in the United States of America
Dover Publications, Inc., 31 East 2nd Street, Mineola, N.Y. 11501

Introduction

The charming hand-colored fashion plates which appear so picturesque to our sophisticated eyes were the last word in fashion reportage in their day. Unlike their predecessors in the 16th to the 18th centuries, which depicted the distinctive national garb worn in the countries of Europe and Africa, the 19th-century plates were meant to forecast fashion, not to document it. As the medium by which the latest styles were disseminated to the public, they played a significant role in the development of the fashion industry.

Fashion news, read as faithfully a century ago as it is today, was sought after so avidly that between 1840 and 1870 over one hundred European periodicals that published fashion, either French or with color plates imported from France, made their appearance. A privileged few Americans actually made semi-annual forays to Paris for the purpose of replenishing their wardrobes, but most women had their clothes made up locally or sewed their own, relying unquestioningly on the fashion bulletins provided by these magazines.

American journals, each claiming to be the first to present the newest styles, catered to this Francomania. Beginning with *Graham's American Monthly Magazine of Literature, Art and Fashion*, in 1826, edited for a time by none other than Edgar Allan Poe, and *Godey's Lady's Book* in 1830, each professed to be the only publication in direct communication with Paris via its own correspondent, while blatantly issuing unauthorized engravings of French fashion plates. A few journals such as *Harper's Bazar* had agreements with European publishers, but piracy was rampant. Figures from several plates were sometimes combined, and details of dress changed with impunity. The American illustrations often appeared as much as a year after the European originals. Whether the intent was to dissemble or merely to Americanize can only be surmised, but American ingenuity in adapting models from foreign journals was truly amazing as well as amusing in its naïveté.

Godey's Lady's Book, virtually synonymous with fashion in the mid-19th century, appears to have been the longest lived and best loved of the American publications, remaining in existence from July 1830 until August 1898. A testimonial on its cover for July 1861, conveys an idea of the affection it commanded: "Godey is chaste in style, beautiful in sentiment, noble in thought, and well calculated to call out all the ennobling virtues of the human heart. No cottage, no palace, no home, however humble or magnificent, is furnished without the *Lady's Book*," a statement borne out by the fact that it reached an unprecedented circulation of 150,000 during the 1860s. Even Scarlett O'Hara was to declare the Civil War a great inconvenience, in no small measure because, as she was vexed to discover, it prevented her from receiving her copy of *Godey's*, which was published in the Union stronghold of Philadephia.

The editor of *Godey's Lady's Book* was the indomitable Sara Josepha Hale, who held the post from 1837 to 1878, succeeding Louis A. Godey, who founded the magazine in 1830 and functioned as both editor and publisher until 1837 when he purchased *The Ladie's Magazine*, edited by Mrs. Hale, in order to obtain her services. The first female editor in the United States, Mrs. Hale was a widow with five children. A true daughter of the republic, her chief interest lay in using the printed page as a forum to champion women's rights. She campaigned for higher education for women, helped to shape the policy and curriculum of Vassar College, urged the admission of women to medical schools, advocated the retention of their property rights after marriage, dignified homemaking with the term "domestic science," and editorialized about these subjects on numerous occasions. Among her forward-thinking concepts were day nurseries for the children of working mothers, public playgrounds, and the establishment of schools for the study of nursing. She was instrumental in the granting of landmark status to Mount Vernon, raising funds for the completion of the Bunker Hill monument, and was responsible for the Presidental proclamation declaring Thanksgiving a national holiday. A prolific author, her most famous work is surely *Mary Had a Little Lamb*.

In the firm belief that fashion news was a mark of the European aristocracy and had no place in America, Mrs. Hale refused at the outset to print such frivolity. However, according to the feminist publication, the *Lily*, even frontier women delighted in "furbelows and flounces," while foreign visitors were constantly amazed at the attention paid to clothes in America. Charles Dickens wrote,"How the ladies dress. What fluttering of ribbons and silk tassels, and displays of cloaks with gaudy hoods and linings!" Perhaps, cognizant of the fact that even the mill girls in Lowell, Massachusetts all subscribed to *Godey's* (*American Beauty*, Lois Banner, 1984), Mrs. Hale conceded that "our whole population is swayed by the reigning mode" and "even the poor must be in fashion," and announced that henceforth some reproductions of French plates would appear in *Godey's*. Nevertheless, she remained outspoken about the slavish manner in which American women followed Paris, declaring that elaborate French fashion did not "answer any exigence in our own affairs." Casting a jaundiced eye across the ocean, Mrs. Hale proclaimed: "Our engraving of the 'Fashions'. . . is not given as a pattern for imitation, but as a study for each reader to examine and decide how far this costume is appropriate to her own figure, face and circumstances. This exercise of individual taste is sadly neglected by our fair countrywomen. We seem willing to adopt almost any and every frippery ornament invented by French and English milliners in order to dispose of old or antiquated materials to the 'universal Yankee nation'. The refined and elegant women of Paris and London would not wear such things . . ." In agreement with her friend, educator Emma Willard, who founded the Troy Female Seminary in 1831, she viewed the French as "chaste and correct," not "finical and dashing," in their manner of dress. Another member of this accomplished circle, Harriet Beecher Stowe, a close friend of Mrs. Hale, who published some of her earliest work, declared passionately, "When a nice little American girl adopts every unnatural fashion that comes from foreign circles—she is in bad taste because she does not represent either her character, her education, nor her good points. It requires only an army of girls to declare independence in America and save us from the tyranny of French actresses and ballet-dancers. Forward girls! You yet can, if you will, save the republic!" Despite such disavowals, *Godey's* constantly published blatant, although vastly delayed, re-engravings of highly styled French fashion, and by the 1860s was reporting blithely on the whims of the Empress Eugenie: "As the empress is decidedly in favor of short dresses for promenade and travelling purposes, we willingly follow her example, and invite attention to a few of the latest styles. . . ." (October 1867).

Peterson's Magazine, for many years *Godey's* chief rival, was founded in 1842; it was similar in format and, like *Godey's*, was published in Philadelphia. In 1863 it claimed to be the cheapest magazine with the "largest circulation of any ladies' periodical in the United States, or even the world," actually surpassing *Godey's* for a time. Not in the least bound by Mrs. Hale's scruples, nor outraged by French dominance of fashion, it devoted as much space to attire as its competitor, boasting, "The fashion department is admitted, by all conversant with such matters, to excel that of any contemporary. The arrangements for *Peterson* are such that all patterns are received in advance. Other magazines continually publish fashions as new which we have published months before. The latest Paris, London, Philadelphia and New York fashions are faithfully reported . . ." Every month a tinted illustration entitled "Les Modes Parisiennes" was featured, apparently utilizing plates from *Le Petit Courrier des Dames*, which employed some of the finest French fashion illustrators of the day. *Godey's* presumably used its own artists to re-engrave French plates, accounting for the relative lack of grace when comparing, often the same figures, with *Peterson's*.

The hand-colored, steel-engraved plates often depicted fashion in anecdotal settings. These genre scenes are, in addition to depicting the last word in feminine attire, a visual history of the social events of their day. *Peterson's* even titled its plates, e.g. "The Reception," "Baby's Levee," "The Picture Gallery," and "An Afternoon Musicale."

In keeping with its mission of instruction, *Godey's* editorialized on its August 1845 colored engraving of a lady in a dressing gown with a little girl and a baby. "Our readers will notice a striking improvement in the style of our recent fashion plates. We give, this month, the latest fashion for ladies and children, in the form of a domestic scene, which serves at once to exhibit the latest fancy in dress, and the most recent improvements in the form of the cradle, easy chair, foot-cushion, & c. [*sic*] Where fine touches of art can be thrown in 'after the fashion', we hold it our duty to see that it is done."

Godey's featured hand-tinted fashion plates from the outset, making sure that its readers were aware of the extra expense incurred on their behalf: "We state an incontrovertible fact, that the *mere colouring* of the prints costs us *nearly three thousand dollars per annum*, and gives employment to twenty females constantly throughout the year." (August 1839) Prior to 1850, when the magazine dealt with fashion it sometimes omitted descriptions of the clothing, while the fashion column appeared sporadically, due no doubt in large measure to Mrs. Hale's reluctance to encourage such superficiality. Like *Peterson's*, *Godey's* published poetry, fiction in the form of short stories and serials, and "embellishments," usually sentimental engravings suitable for framing, printed on one side only, as well as needlework projects and book reviews. Additional apparel and accessories appeared in black and white, an "extension" or fold-out plate being a feature of every issue in *Godey's* from 1861 and adopted by *Peterson's* a few years later. Black and white illustrations of "cottages," or slightly grander "villas" with floor plans, as well as sheet music, advice on household management, child care, gardening, and editorials endorsing causes dear to the editor's heart completed the contents.

Mrs. Hale's continuing ambivalence toward "la mode" while boasting of her book's timeliness, is obvious in a description of a cape in July 1837: "This we give, not for its beauty exactly, but to convince our fair readers that we give them the newest fashions, whilst still only adopted by the French court, consequently months before such articles are to be seen commonly worn in Paris, or displayed in the shop windows." In a February 1839 column called "Fashion," under the heading "Editor's Table," decrying the futility of denying fashion, she remarked that "we are still rocked in fashionable cradles, and buried in fashionable coffins—and in all the intermediate scenes of our existence we feel the influence, and acknowledge the supremacy of the grand enchantress." She went on to say that even if "we flatter ourselves that we are not partakers in this species of idolatry," everyone is anxious to conform to the fashion approved by his or her circle and "some attention to fashion is not, in itself, unwise nor injudicious." Later that year, immediately below a discourse on the progress of institutions of higher learning for women, the fashion column reported the latest news in accessories, fabrics, and coiffures. In 1840, a feature describing both color and black-and-white plates, as well as information on the latest mode, was introduced. Called "Chitchat on Fashions," it could be found thenceforth from time to time, occasionally informing the reader where the items described might be purchased.

On an even more helpful note, in 1852, the magazine instituted a buying service. A notice to "Lady Subscribers" read,

Having had frequent applications for the purchase of jewelry, millinery, etc., by ladies living at a distance, The Editress of the Fashion Department will hereafter execute commissions for any who may desire it, with the charge of a small percentage for the time and research required. Spring and autumn bonnets, materials for dresses, jewelry, envelops, hair-work, worsteds, children's wardrobes, mantillas, and mantelets, will be chosen with a view to economy, as well as taste; and boxes or packages forwarded by express to any part of the country. For the last, distinct directions must be given. . . . No order will be attended to unless the money is first received. Neither the Editor nor Publisher will be acccountable for losses that may occur in remitting.

When goods are ordered, the fashions that prevail here govern the purchase; therefore, no articles will be taken back. When the goods are sent, the transaction must be considered final.

Only outerwear, underclothing and accessories were available ready-made; hence the apparel illustrations were accompanied by minutely detailed descriptions of colors and materials (much abridged in this Dover volume) even when the drawings were in black and white, providing an indispensible guide for the seamstress. On occasion, alternative color combinations and, for the sake of economy, fabrics were suggested. If a woman cared to be à la mode, no matter where she lived, she could commission *Godey's* fashion editress to purchase fabric for her, and with the latest plate as a guide she could make up the goods in one of the models pictured. Descriptions of hats, headdresses and hairstyles completed the fashion information.

While ever cognizant of the role played by fashion in selling a woman's magazine, Mrs. Hale's concern with health and her fervent belief in exercise for women "to counteract nervousness and invalidism, not to make athletes," and that "no false notions of gentility or propriety . . . should deter any woman from engaging in sports or exercises that will increase the size of her lungs, and fill them with an abundance of pure health-giving and life-sustaining air"(January 1860), led to her opposition to tight-lacing and was one reason why the French fashions in *Godey's* were "Americanized:" "American ladies have not yet given up waists of a respectable and natural size, a part of the figure the French *artistes des modes* sometimes omit altogether . . ." Curiously, in spite of her outspokenness about the importance of comfort and health, she never promoted reform dress, viewing the Bloomer costume in particular as a senseless statement which was to become identified with radical women's groups. In 1878, *Godey's* bemoaned the return of the small waist: "This fashion will tend to fill doctors' pockets with considerable rapidity, and help to people cemeteries in an ever-increasing ratio. It is all very well that medical men and undertakers should earn their living, but unavoidable diseases gives them ample opportunities of doing so, as far as we can judge." Even bonnets, never intended as the most practical of accessories, did not escape the health conscious eye of Mrs. Hale. In a winter issue, commenting on the absence of bonnet strings, she expressed concern for "the ears, left unprotected by even a suspicion of ribbon, a shadow of lace, or a shading of hair," wondering how "their rosy tips can 'bide the pelting of the pitiless storm'" (February 1869).

The years of Mrs. Hale's editorship encompassed enormous changes in fashion. The multiple petticoats supporting the full skirts of the thirties and forties were replaced in 1856 by the crinoline, an open cage of metal hoops graduated in circumference and held at intervals by vertical tapes attached to a waistband, which allowed for skirts of even greater width at the hem, as well as increased comfort for the wearer. After reaching their maximum circumference in 1860, skirts began to flatten in front and move rearward. The leg-of-mutton sleeves of the 1830s had shrunk to the constricting, tight-fitting arm coverings of the forties, flaring into a bell in the following decade and sprouting sheer undersleeves from forearm to wrist, while delicate chemisettes covered the bosom as necklines descended. By 1870, the crinoline had been superseded by a bustle of the same construction or by stiff horsehair ruffles, and the enormous quantities of fabric swept back in the latter sixties were gathered and bunched up behind over these scaffoldings. Costumes were often made of two shades of the same color, with elaborate matching trim of another fabric, often velvet. By the seventies, two fabrics as well as two colors were the general rule, and hardly an edge escaped embellishment by velvet, lace, pleats, or a combination of all three. While intense hues were favored for afternoon and house dresses, somber elephant gray and brown were considered appropriate for street wear; and the penchant for pink, often in combination with white and sometimes tulle and flowers, made it the undisputed favorite for formal occasions, turning ballrooms into paintings by Tissot. Hats sat atop enormous masses of hair curled and puffed in a manner rivaling the dresses below. By mid-decade the bustle was modified and the rigid cuirass bodice appeared. As it continued to lengthen, the silhouette pared down, culminating in the fashionably erect, pencil-slim figure of 1880, the train virtually nonexistent, with the entire torso encased in an armor-like sheath, often severely tailored, from shoulder to knee.

As colors became stronger the demeanor of the ladies in the fashion plates followed suit, becoming more assertive and less shy. Color as well as cut was directly influenced by Paris, hence such colors as "Bismarck," a kind of brown, "magenta," and "Metternich green" (after the fashionable wife of the Austrian ambassador to the French court). In 1869, according to *Godey's*, "Costumes cannot be too gay or too picturesque; many of the street costumes are exact copies from some of the old painters" (May 1869). Myriad borrowings can be detected in the fashion vocabulary of those years, from 16th-century

slashing and puffing, 17th-century off-the-shoulder bertha décolletages, and Marie Antoinette polonaises. Even the lone child who appeared each month in *Godey's* color plate, dressed in Vandyke costumes and Marie Antoinette fichus, was not exempt from this unbridled eclecticism.

Technology was responsible in no small measure for many of these fashion changes. The sewing machine, with increasingly sophisticated attachments, enabled the seamstress to tuck, pleat, ruffle, puff, quilt, embroider, and embellish to her heart's content. *Godey's* declared, "With regard to trimming, fancy may indulge herself to the fullest extent; the modiste is allowed any extravagance which her inspiration may dictate" (October 1867). Lace edgings, once painstakingly made by hand with needle or bobbin, could now be replicated mechanically by the yard. Fancy braids and pipings were available in numerous widths and designs, while synthetic dyes permitted a broad color spectrum, accounting in part for the rage for strident hues such as "arsenic green," harsh pinks, and the intense violets and purples that owed their existence to mauveine, the first aniline dyestuff, discovered by Sir William Perkin in 1856. As spinning and weaving looms increased in speed, greater quantities of textiles were produced, while the jacquard system permitted complex patterns and textures. All these innovations were employed to advantage in the exuberant excesses of surface decoration that are a hallmark of the latter part of the 19th century. By 1900, stiff velvets and damasks had given way to frothy Edwardian chiffons and furbelows, but the concept of unadorned simplicity and subtlety as virtual synonyms for elegance would not be imagined until Gabrielle Chanel appeared on the scene a half century later. To modern eyes accustomed to minimal amounts of fabric and ornament, the miles of flounces and bows bedecking *Godey's* fashion plates make them appear no less antiquated than the styles of earlier centuries, evoking an aura of romance and nostalgia.

In 1877, Louis Godey died, and in December, the ninety-year-old Mrs. Hale, after forty years at the masthead, wrote her last editorial. *Godey's*, now only one of many competing American women's journals, was sold the following year. By the 1880s the field numbered eighteen, including the *Ladies' Home Journal, Good Housekeeping, Harper's Bazar,* founded as a weekly in 1867, the *Queen of Fashion* (later *McCall's*), and the *Delineator,* from 1873. *Bazar* employed a larger format and devoted a greater percentage of space to fashion than either *Godey's* or *Peterson's,* while the *Queen of Fashion* and the *Delineator* were primarily fashion publications with an emphasis on the promotion of their paper dress patterns. In the eighties, *Godey's* abandoned hand-colored steel engravings and adopted mechanically-printed color plates, which *Peterson's* was to do somewhat later, both eliminating all color by 1892. In spite of *Godey's* attempts at modernization by introducing photographic material, it appeared somewhat outmoded, and, while presumably still read by a loyal but dwindling elderly population, circulation fell well below that of the newer magazines. Perhaps due to the absence of Mrs. Hale's sure editorial hand, the quality of the magazine began to decline. After almost seventy years, *Godey's* ceased publication just two years short of the 20th century. However, the groundwork laid by Sarah Josepha Hale, arising from her passionate beliefs in higher education and women's rights, was in large measure directly responsible for the improved status and virtually unlimited opportunities available to women today. While her language was stilted and her demure paper ladies dressed in cumbersome old-fashioned apparel, her convictions and concepts remain as fresh and modern as they were when she first proposed them in the pages of *Godey's* over a century ago.

Notes on Plates

PLATE 1. MAY 1841. "The coloured plate in this number is not offered as a fashion plate, but the dress is simply beautiful and very appropriate to the season. The lady appears to have been favoured with a very early copy of the May number."

PLATE 2. FEBRUARY 1838 AND JULY 1838. *Fig. a.* Pale fawn dress and matching "peasant fashion" cape edged with silk fringe. Tight sleeves with fancy silk trimming; cord and tassel to match the belt. Matching silk bonnet. *Fig. b.* Morning dress of Jaconet muslin. Tight sleeves with a single puff above the elbow; lace ruffle at wrist. The skirt has a deep flounce. Plain body crossed in front, showing a cambric kerchief, with a lace frill. *Fig. c.* Yellow poult-de-soie hat. Gros de Naples dress; low corsage, tight sleeves, three flounces at hem. Arab mantelet or shawl of cashmere, satin, or twisted silk. The garland is embroidered in floss silks or worsted. *Fig. d.* Gros de Naples capote. Cashmere dress, with a single deep flounce; mantelet of filet, trimmed with blonde.

PLATE 3. NOVEMBER 1838 AND AUGUST 1838. *Fig. a.* Poult-de-soie dress. Tight corsage, plain sleeves. The flounce at the hem is headed by a bouillon. Square satin shawl, trimmed with white blonde. Hat of poult-de-soie, trimming of tulle, square net. Hair in ringlets. A fall of lace over the corsage, fastened by a large brooch. *Fig. b.* Dinner or evening dress of mousselline de laine embroidered in bouquets in tambour work and twisted silks. Tight corsage without a point. Long, full sleeves, tiny plaits on the shoulder, satin ribbon bow with a second small bow on wrist. The skirt has two flounces. Dress cap of blonde, with green or pink ribbons; long blonde lappets in lieu of strings; hair in smooth bands. Black satin shoes; white kid gloves. *Fig. c.* Evening dress of tulle over white satin. Corsage à pointe, with three seams in front, each ornamented with a wreath of flowers. Short, tight sleeves, in small flat folds or plaits, with a wide frill of tulle. The skirt has a deep flounce, headed by a puffed trimming of white and colored gauze; similar trimming around the sleeve, bosom, and the guimpe, worn inside the corsage. Hair, in nattes à la Clotilde, very low at each side of the face; the braid at back retains lappets of blonde. A wreath of roses and drooping flowers on the head. Half-long white kid gloves, trimmed with a tulle ruche. White satin shoes. *Fig. d.* Evening dress of crepe over satin. Corsage à pointe. A wreath of flowers in place of the gauze trimming on the other dress. In all other respects the toilette is similar to *Fig. c.*

PLATE 4. APRIL 1840. *Fig. a.* Dress of white cambric; changeable silk apron trimmed with black lace. Tight corsage with a matching tucker trimmed with pink bows. The back hair is worn so low behind that it touches the back of the neck, being pulled at the very roots of the hair, forming the figure eight. *Fig. b.* Changeable silk dress. Tight corsage crossed in front. Bishop sleeves with four bands at the top, each trimmed with a button; the skirt is trimmed with five narrow flounces. Straw hat. *Fig. c.* White figured muslin dress, V-shaped corsage. The skirt trimmed down the front and hem with three tucks. Silk hat.

PLATE 5. SEPTEMBER 1840. *Fig. a.* Evening dress with corsage à pointe, two net and blonde flounces at hem, single flounces at elbows and wide neckline. *Figs. b–d.* Day dresses with trimmed bonnets.

PLATE 6. DECEMBER 1840. *Fig. a.* Dress suitable for evening visits. *Fig. b.* Bride's dress. *Figs. c* and *d.* Ball dresses. "There is little change in the fashions during the winter months."

PLATE 7. FEBRUARY 1841. *Fig. a.* Fawn-colored silk dress with front opening, worn with large square wool shawl. *Fig. b.* White silk evening gown; black taffeta mantelet. *Fig. c.* Green silk skirt with white organdy chemisette. *Fig. d.* Changeable silk dress; shawl of red, brown, green, and white stripes.

PLATE 8. JUNE 1841. *Fig. a.* Fine white cashmere dress, two rows of colored silk floss embroidery and tucks around bottom of skirt. Hat of white poult-de-soie. *Fig. b.* Blue dress with three lace-edged tucks. Low-necked corsage. The sleeves have four puffs. "This dress is very beautiful, and is the prevailing fashion." Caising bonnet. *Fig. c.* Colored skirt; white waist, sleeve gaged at the top, the neckline edged with a puff. Straw bonnet. *Fig. d.* Solid-colored silk, deep flounce, full sleeves; trimming at the top of the sleeve is the same as the flounce. Collar of quilled lace. Caising bonnet.

PLATE 9. SEPTEMBER 1841. *Fig. a.* Plain silk with tight waist, low neck, and full sleeves with a band at the wrist. Skirt open from the waist, trimmed with fine piping. Hat of rice straw. Straw-colored gloves; embroidered handkerchief. *Fig. b.* Striped silk dress with a plain waist and low neck, trimmed with a broad lace. Skirt has two flounces. Matching scarf. Silk hat. *Fig. c.* White muslin robe, colored silk embroidery. Low corsage with a deep yoke of shirred muslin. Full sleeves. Bonnet of white poult-de-soie. *Fig. d.* Dress of dark silk with a low neck; waist and skirt edged with a ruche in a novel manner. Matching shawl, edged with lace. Crepe bonnet.

PLATE 10. MARCH 1842. *Fig. a.* Walking dress of poult-de-soie; skirt trimmed with two broad bias tucks headed with a narrow fringe matching the dress; body and sleeves tight; velvet scarf, piped in small vandykes of satin; matching small collar. Satin bonnet. *Fig. b.* Satin, with a velvet facing, cut in rounded points, edged with satin; the body high, finished by a velvet collar. Tight sleeves, finished at the top with two velvet epaulettes. Chapeau of pale blue velvet, with lace lappets. *Fig. c.* Gros de Naples dress; high plaited corsage; small bishop sleeves finished with a narrow band, the cap tucked; the waist finished with a belt. Skirt trimmed with tucks, à la discretion. Silk bonnet. *Fig. d.* Walking dress of poult-de-soie, the skirt trimmed with a wide bias tuck; black moiré scarf with piping, trimmed with rich lace. Silk bonnet.

PLATE 11. MAY 1842. *Fig. a.* Gray satin dress. Tight corsage has three rows of trimming or puffing from shoulder to waist. Full sleeves, taken in at the top of the arm and also above the wrist, with narrow lace ruffles falling over the edge of the glove. Small bonnet of drawn lace. *Fig. b.* Drawn capote of moss green or blue crepe. Dress of nankeen silk. Tight corsage, sleeves are similar to those of the other dress. Gauze scarf, lace collar. *Fig. c.* Promenade dress of cambric muslin. Corsage fastens in back. The skirt has three enormous lace-edged tucks. White crepe lisse bonnet. Hair in bands. *Fig. d.* Dress of striped gros de Naples. Tight corsage, open in front to the waist. Sleeves with turned-up cuffs. Lace frill at neck. Skirt has nine tucks. Yellow crepe hat. The hair is in bands.

PLATE 12. FEBRUARY 1843. *Fig. a.* "A fashionable cloak of strong woolen cloth, unprepossessing in its appearance, but very durable and warm." Matching fringe. *Fig. b.* "The latest French fashion, hardly yet introduced among us. . . . A graceful garment, it will be very popular." The material is merino, made to fit the figure, confined at the waist with a cord and tassel; Hungary sleeves; short skirt, trimmed with a cord and lined with colored silk. *Fig. c.* Blue velvet mantilla cloak, trimmed with swansdown. Velvet hat. *Fig. d.* Striped silk dress, pointed corsage. Fanciful piping down sides of skirt. Velvet bonnet. *Fig. e.* Lavender silk coat dress. Moderate size cape, tight sleeves, narrow belt. White velvet bonnet.

PLATE 13. MARCH 1843. "The Fashions in this number do not require any description. They are beautifully simple. The children's dresses we think must please."

PLATE 14. JULY 1843. *Fig. a.* Equestrienne. *Figs. b–d.* Summer dresses.

PLATE 15. JANUARY 1843. *Fig. a.* Dress of thibet merino with six braided tucks. Down the front is a large tuck, trimmed with braid. *Fig. b.* Dress of gros de Brazil, with seven flounces, each edged with a bias fold. *Fig. c.* Dress of embroidered white tarletane muslin. *Fig. d.* Open dress of Altapacca poplin, trimmed with silk cord. *Fig. e.* Dress of Turkish satin, pleats or folds down the front, caught at intervals with satin knots or clasps. Neck and sleeves trimmed with rich lace. Headdress of satin ribbon and flowers.

PLATE 16. NOVEMBER 1843. *Figs. a., b.,* and *d.* Cloth mantles. *Fig. c.* Ermine mantle with matching muff.

PLATE 17. JANUARY 1844. "Fancy Dresses of Four Nations, which we present this month. They are coloured in magnificent style, and form an attractive feature in the Pictorial Department of the Lady's Book."

PLATE 18. MARCH 1844. *Fig. a.* Promenade dress of sea green pekin silk; very full skirt trimmed with two broad bias bands of green velvet. Tight corsage, closed down the front with a velvet band. Plain sleeve, loose over the elbow, where it is faced with a broad velvet band. Undersleeves of batiste, a tulle ruche at the throat. Capote of green velvet. *Fig. b.* Promenade dress of lilac satin; the skirt has three deep tucks, each headed with a narrow fluted frill. Tight high corsage. Close-fitting sleeves, the top ornamented with a cap, edged with a fluted frill. Black velvet bonnet. *Fig. c.* Shaded blue pekin silk. The skirt bordered with one immense ruffle, with a fluted trimming. Tight-fitting corsage and tight sleeves with a cap, also trimmed with a fluting. *Fig. d.* Walking dress of French gray silk; full skirt, trimmed with bows and buckles; the waist made to lap, ornamented with three broad folds; tight sleeves, finished with a bracelet. Bonnet of white chip.

PLATE 19. 1845. *Figs. a., d.,* and *e.* Ladies' dresses. *Fig. b.* Boy's suit. *Fig. c.* Girl's dress, worn with bonnet and net mitts.

PLATE 20. OCTOBER 1845. The Polka Fashions.

PLATE 21. APRIL 1845. Evening dresses. "We do not consider it necessary to go into a detailed description of the manner of making the dresses, as the plate is so distinct and the dresses so beautifully and clearly defined that any mantua-maker's apprentice could make them."

PLATE 22. APRIL 1850 AND DECEMBER 1850. *Fig. a.* Opera dress of light silk or turc satin, low neck, short sleeves, and a triple puffing of the material over the skirt, with knots of matching ribbon. Pink satin cloak, ribbon quillings, and a deep flounce of black lace; similar trimming edges the wide sleeves. A hood of black lace over pink silk, fastened lightly under the chin. White kid gloves and a fan. *Fig. b.* Dress of an invalid or convalescent. Robe of embroidered cambric, with a deep flounce and full sleeves. White cashmere dressing gown with rich embroidery, lined with quilted rose silk, tied with a cord at the waist. Morning-cap of India muslin. Embroidered slippers with a small rosette on the instep. *Fig. c.* Purple velvet walking dress; black velvet mantle. The cape has a fringe nearly a quar-

ter of a yard in depth, with a new style of heading. The demi-long sleeves are looped up with knots of the velvet, displaying muslin undersleeves. Small square collar. Close white bonnet. *Fig. d.* Walking-dress of green cashmere. "Jenny Lind" mantilla of claret velvet, with two lace flounces headed by satin piping. At the waist, the mantilla closes from right to left with a row of very small agate buttons. Bonnet of green uncut velvet to match the dress.

PLATE 23. JULY 1850 AND OCTOBER 1854. *Fig. a.* Fashions for Children's Dresses. "We cannot enforce more earnestly than is necessary, perfect simplicity in the dress of children. They are not puppets, made for the display of fine clothes; nor Paris dolls, to be tricked out in the extravagance of the latest fashion. We give a report of what may be worn; but every mother should be guided by her means, her time, and the health of her infant." *Fig. b.* Walking dress of ash-colored brocaded silk, the checks formed by heavy satin stripes a shade darker than the ground. The trimming is a matching broad ribbon. The sleeves open on the forearm, to display flowing sleeves of rich cambric-work. White China shawl, embroidered in colors. Bonnet of rose silk. *Fig. c.* Walking dress of brocade, in a woven striped pattern of vines and flowers. Plain corsage. Short skirt with belt and buckle. Drawn bonnet of dark-green silk.

PLATE 24. SEPTEMBER 1858. *Fig. a.* Carriage dress of rose silk, shot with black; the satin border of the flounces, etc., is also black. Heart-shaped bertha trimmed with fringe; plain corsage. Full undersleeves of white figured Brussels net. White crepe bonnet with a bird-of-paradise plume. *Fig. b.* Evening dress of ashes-of-roses silk. The skirt has three bouillons at the hem, and garlands of roses, foliage, and drooping grass give the effect of a triple skirt. Wreaths finish the bertha and encircle the head. *Fig. c.* Evening dress of white satin, with blonde, and ornaments in gold. Headdress of the same. *Fig. d.* Evening dress of white crepe. The flowers which ornament it are arranged en tablier, or apron fashion; spray of the same flowers to the left of the coiffure. *Fig. e.* Lavender silk dress; the skirt has three flounces. Short opera cloak in rose and white tissue. Pearl comb and loops of pearls in hair.

PLATE 25. OCTOBER 1858. *Fig. a.* Dressing gown of fawn silk or cashmere. Pale blue silk quilting around skirt, on the wide sleeves, and en tablier to a similar band at the neck. Half-high body to show a cambric habit-shirt with a frill at the throat. Puffed muslin undersleeves. Tartan ribbon headdress. *Fig. b.* Walking dress of dark green velvet, with velvet polka spots; trimming of green velvet bands. Velvet and lace bonnet. *Fig. c.* Black moiré dinner dress with double skirt. Upper skirt, corsage, and sleeves trimmed with chenille fringe. Lace headdress. *Fig. d.* Walking dress, suitable for dinner, of fawn silk chiné. Triple skirt, the middle one has quilles of black velvet ribbon on a flat plait; the top one has the effect of a tunic, open in front and trimmed to match corsage and sleeves. Black lace and blue velvet bonnet.

PLATE 26. NOVEMBER 1858. *Fig. a.* Silk carriage dress, very light shade of *groseille.* Skirt trimmed with a deep fringe, the heading heavily netted. Carriage-wrap of brown ladies' cloth, trimmed with bands of embossed velvet ribbon. Pink satin hat. *Fig. b.* Green silk dress with flounces. Velvet mantle with embroidery. Bonnet of straw-colored silk. *Fig. c.* Walking dress of black-and-brown striped silk. Pleated velvet mantle trimmed with four feather ruches and a lace flounce. White satin bonnet. *Fig. d.* Robe of ashes-of-roses silk; green velvet mantle; pink plush hat. *Fig. e.* Blue robe *à quille.* Loose fitting cloth cloak, satin and fringe trim. Bonnet of pale blue plush.

PLATE 27. JULY 1861. *Fig. a.* Robe with three skirts of pink and white tulle, each edged with satin ribbon, over white silk. The upper skirt is open, and the ends are crossed over like a fichu, and fastened by bouquets of waterlilies mingled with blades of grass and sprays of small flowers. Pink satin corselet, surmounted by white tulle, pointed at top and bottom in front; pointed only at the top in back. A wreath of waterlilies with grass encircles the head. *Fig. b.* Zouave jacket of embroidered blue armure silk. White muslin shirt with bouffant sleeves, buttoned by a row of coral buttons or studs, with a small standing collar and cuffs of blue embroidered silk, edged with narrow lace. Skirt of blue armure, trimmed with an embroidered band. Blue velvet waistband, gold embroidery. Coiffure Orientale: a bandeau in gold passementerie, a rosette on each side encircled with gold beads, and pendant gold tassels. *Fig. c.* White grenadine skirt with green bands; waist and overskirt of fine French muslin; shoulder knots and sash of green ribbon; white Leghorn hat. *Fig. d.* Summer habit: buff nankeen skirt, white piqué jacket trimmed with Marseilles buttons, blue necktie, and white straw hat. *Fig. e.* Magenta grenadine skirt over a silk slip; white muslin spencer, made of puffs and inserting, trimmed with magenta ribbons. Coiffure of black lace and daisies. Mathilde gloves.

PLATE 28. SEPTEMBER 1862. *Fig. a.* Violet foulard dress, with three rows of quilled ribbon around the skirt and en tablier. The corsage is trimmed with quilled ribbon in Zouave style. Sash trimmed with a ribbon quilling. *Fig. b.* Green silk dress, trimmed with black velvet sewn around the skirt in diamond form, and graduated up each side, and on corsage and sleeves. Quilted white crepe bonnet, with a black velvet curtain trimmed with white lace. *Fig. c.* Gray poplin dress with a black velvet corselet, trimmed with black velvet in bands, lozenges, and bows. Small lace collar with black velvet bow. *Fig. d.* Pongee home-dress, of the new cuir color. The skirt is trimmed on one side only, with self bands and bows. Coat body, with revers. Chemisette with ruff. *Fig. e.* Ruby silk dinner dress, trimmed with one deep flounce, and en tablier with small flounces edged with lace. The tunic skirt is bordered by a silk ruche. Black velvet sash, with fringes and ruby silk embroidery. Low corsage, trimmed to match the skirt, and worn with a puffed chemisette with flounced sleeves.

PLATE 29. NOVEMBER 1864. *Fig. a.* Skirt of heavy black silk, jacket of white silk, both trimmed with crimson silk bands braided with black. The hair is rolled in front and dressed with crimson velvet and small tufts of flowers. *Fig. b.* Skirt of chocolat-au-lait silk, with streamers of green silk trimmed with black lace. Jacket of black silk grosgrain, trimmed with black velvet and steel buttons. The hair is arranged in a net at the back. Black felt hat. *Fig. c.* Visiting suit of pearl-colored poplin, magenta silk vest. White uncut velvet bonnet. *Fig. d.* Walking suit of cuir poplin, guipure lace, and crochet trimming. The skirt is looped over a petticoat of stripes of blue-and-white merino, trimmed with black velvet. White plush bonnet, purple velvet crown. *Fig. e.* Pearl-colored poplin dress, and puffed waist of white cashmere, trimmed with magenta velvet. Poplin sash trimmed to match. Hair rolled from the face and caught in a net, trimmed with magenta ribbon. *Fig. f.* Purple silk dress, trimmed with black velvet and chenille fringe, simulating a tunic. White corded-silk bonnet, trimmed with jet.

PLATE 30. APRIL 1864. *Fig. a.* Dinner dress of pearl gray silk trimmed with ornaments of gold-colored chenille cord and chenille drop buttons. *Fig. b.* Evening dress of heavy white corded silk, trimmed with black lace leaves. *Fig. c.* Child's costume. Red Riding Hood sack of scarlet flannel; dress of checked silk, trimmed with Imperial blue silk. *Fig. d.* Walking dress of smoke gray poplin with trimmings of rich passementerie; white chip hat with scarlet velvet and white plumes. *Fig. e.* Gown of lilac silk with a fancy lace design on the skirt; sash of white silk trimmed with black velvet. *Fig. f.* Walking dress of brown alpaca with black braid trim; fancy plaid wrap with chenille fringe.

PLATE 31. JUNE 1864. *Fig. a.* Costume for a wedding reception. Ruby silk dress, figured with black velvet. Mantle of white yak lace, trimmed with camel's hair tassels. White crepe bonnet, with a fall of point lace over the brim à la Marie Stuart. White parasol with marabou fringe. *Fig. b.* Black silk dinner dress trimmed with chenille tassels. Tight bodice and sleeves trimmed with black velvet and chenille fringe. Velvet stomacher with white piping, scalloped silk tablier. Striped silk underskirt. Straw hat. *Fig. c.* Dress of white grenadine, figured with black. Triangular black-and-white ruffled silk insets on skirt, matching ruchings on corsage and on broad black silk band at waist. Leghorn hat. *Fig. d.* Cuir percale suit, with bands stamped to resemble guipure lace. Straw hat trimmed with poppies. *Fig. e.* Imperial blue silk dress, box-plaited ruffle at hem, headed by a quilling. Fancy trim of black lace insertion and velvet on skirt panels. Low neck, short-sleeved corsage with Figaro-style jacket of black lace. Black lace coiffure.

PLATE 32. JANUARY 1865. *Fig. a.* Purple corded-silk dress. The skirt is trimmed, en tablier, with bands of white plush and mother-of-pearl buttons, edged with a fluted ruffle. The corsage has a deep tail in back, and is trimmed to match the skirt. Curtainless bonnet of puffed white silk. *Fig. b.* Cuir silk dress, trimmed with thibet fringe. White velvet bonnet, trimmed with plumes, loops of green velvet, pink daisies, and blonde lace. Black velvet shawl embroidered with beads. *Fig. c.* White corded-silk dress. The skirt has a crepe flounce, looped over with bands of white ribbon. The corsage is made with deep points both back and front; sleeves trimmed to match the skirt. Illusion veil, caught in front with a bunch of orange blossoms; the hair is rolled from the face, and arranged in a waterfall at the back. *Fig. d.* White satin dress, trimmed with a point appliqué lace flounce, headed by a quilling of white ribbon and chenille tassels. Illusion veil. The hair is rolled from the face, and dressed with a tuft of orange blossoms. *Fig. e.* Pink silk dress, trimmed with chenille fringe and a quilling of ribbon. Guimpe of white muslin, with long sleeves edged with a muslin ruff. *Fig. f.* Bright blue cashmere morning-robe, trimmed with white plush bands edged with black velvet. Underskirt tucked to the waist. White muslin waist, embroidered trim. Lace cap.

PLATE 33. APRIL 1865. *Fig. a.* Dinner dress of ruby silk, with a box-plaited ruff at the hem, bound with black, and headed by a quilling of heavy black silk. The corsage is trimmed with a small cape, with a narrow ruffle. Cape and sleeves are trimmed with quillings of black silk. *Fig. b.* Child's dress of white alpaca, edged with a narrow fluted ruffle and seven rows of blue silk piping. The point, bretelles, and sash are all of blue silk. Guimpe with long, puffed, muslin sleeves. Boots of blue lasting. *Fig. c.* Fawn-colored spring poplin, open at back and front, showing a skirt of blue silk. Epaulettes, cuffs, and the band around the neck are also of blue silk. White silk drawn bonnet. *Fig. d.* Green silk dress, trimmed with thick cording around the skirt, graduated up the front, and on the sleeves. Leghorn hat. *Fig. e.* Spring suit, of light cuir mohair, with buttons to match. The hair is caught in a net of heavy green chenille; leghorn hat. *Fig. f.* Purple silk suit, trimmed at the hem with two rows of narrow ribbon quilled with rosettes between. The same trimming is around the paletot and up the back. White straw hat.

PLATE 34. MARCH 1865. *Fig. a.* Spring checked silk, trimmed with blue silk, arranged in a fancy design. The corsage is trimmed in jacket style in front, and has a long coat tail at the back. Coat sleeve slit up the outside, trimmed with blue silk. White silk bonnet with an ostrich feather. *Fig. b.* Child's dress of white figured alpaca, scalloped and bound with scarlet velvet; scarlet chenille embroidery. Full loops of scarlet velvet are on the sleeves and at the back of the dress. *Fig. c.* Black silk circle, trimmed with large jet beads and narrow black velvet piping. Bonnet of green silk, trimmed with black and white lace. *Fig. d.* Morning-robe of light cuir poplin, turned back with green silk facing, and trimmed around the skirt and on the corsage with a plait of chenille cord. Fine muslin, trimmed with a worked ruffle and rows of inserting. Chemisette of Valenciennes inserting and puffs of muslin. Fancy muslin cap. *Fig. e.* Pearl-colored spring poplin, trimmed on the skirt with two rows of Solferino velvet, with long velvet loops. Wide velvet belt, fancy gilt buckle. Coat sleeve bound with Solferino velvet, and trimmed with an epaulette of loops. White drawn bonnet. *Fig. f.* Walking dress of purple silk, with matching paletot. Both are trimmed with wide black velvet ribbon, finished with long chenille pendants. White drawn silk bonnet.

PLATE 35. NOVEMBER 1865. *Fig. a.* Promenade suit for a young lady. Dress and sack of violet poplin, ornamented by thick silk cord. The sack is loose in front, and cut into the figure in the back. Linen collar and sleeves. White felt hat. Gloves of undressed kid. *Fig. b.* Golden brown striped silk dress, trimmed with bias pieces of plain silk, arrranged in a square and finished with large velvet buttons. Black velvet paletot ornamented with bretelles and sash ends, trimmed with gimp and bugles. The hair is rolled à la Pompadour. The coiffure is two rolls of golden brown velvet. *Fig. c.* Dress of blue reps, trimmed with black silk and tassels. Cuir velvet bonnet. *Fig. d.* Dress and sack of gray linsey, trimmed with quillings and bands of green velvet. The sack skirt is turned back with revers of green silk. The green belt is fastened with a pearl buckle. Gray felt hat. *Fig. e.* Little girl's dress of magenta silk, trimmed with bands of white silk crossed by black velvet, and finished with a black-and-white chenille fringe. The corsage has a white silk vest in front and a long tail at the back. The hair is rolled from the face and arranged in plaits at the back, with black velvet bows. *Fig. f.* Purple silk gored skirt, with scallops edged with velvet ribbon headed by black beads, on the edge and up each side. Velvet jacket, trimmed with jet fringe. Velvet sash and bag, richly ornamented with beads and bugles. Velvet and beads in fancy designs ornament the front of the dress.

PLATE 36. JUNE 1865. *Fig. a.* Morning costume for a watering-place. Dress of white alpaca gored à l'Imperatrice, and trimmed with rose velvet ribbon and goat-hair tassels. The hair is à la Pompadour, with a coiffure of black silk net, with large beads and a velvet coronet. *Fig. b.* Afternoon dress for a young lady, of blue grenadine, cross-barred and figured with black. A waved trimming of pale blue silk with black lace, chenille tassels, and gimp on skirt and bertha. The low corsage is pointed, showing a chemisette of thin muslin puffs and Valenciennes inserting. The bertha crosses in front, and ties in back with long ends. *Fig. c.* Promenade dress and mantle of brown alpaca, trimmed with black velvet and ball fringe. The jacket is Señorita shape, quite short in back. The dress is looped over a skirt of white lustre, trimmed with scarlet braid and fluted ruffles. Brown straw hat. *Fig. d.* Morning costume for a watering-place. A gored dress of white piqué, trimmed with a fluted ruffle. The overdress is Violine cambric, trimmed with a fluted ruffle and a gay border. A fanchon of black lace is thrown over the head and tied under the chin. *Fig. e.* A dress and shawl of white organdy muslin, striped with black. The skirt is scalloped on the edge and bound with scarlet braid; scarlet sash. The sleeves are scalloped with red, and trimmed with small pearl buttons. White chip hat. White silk parasol, covered with black lace.

PLATE 37. MAY 1865. *Fig. a.* Light Russian gray silk, with blue silk bands edged with black lace. Gray silk tunic skirt with blue silk in front, quite long in back, cut in points in front and trimmed with blue-and-gray fringe. The corsage has revers,

trimmed with black lace. Fancy black-and-white lace cap. *Fig. b.* Coeur-de-melon silk dress, trimmed with a deep puff on the skirt, with scarlet velvet bands and loops. Guimpe has long puffed sleeves of French muslin and Valenciennes inserting. *Fig. c.* Buff poplinette dress, thick chenille cord trim. The skirt is edged with a fluted ruffle of black silk sewn in festoons. The hair is rolled from the face, and a bunch of curls conceals the front parting. *Fig. d.* Green spring silk figured with black. The skirt is open on each side, and a gore of white silk let in. Each side of the gore is trimmed with velvet braid in a Grecian pattern. Tight corsage with square tail faced with white silk. Purple silk bonnet. *Fig. e.* Violine silk dinner dress, buttoned down the back with velvet buttons. Skirt is edged with a plaiting of black chenille. Corsage trimmed with chenille and gimp ornaments. Matching petticoat with lace flounce.

PLATE 38. OCTOBER 1867. *Fig. a.* Walking suit of dark blue poplin, with a plaited ruffle at the hem, caught by a black velvet band. The upper skirt and revers are trimmed and faced with velvet. The corsage is cut with a fancy basquine trimmed to suit the skirt. Gray velvet hat. *Fig. b.* Home dress of black silk richly embroidered en tablier, with a long train. In front, the skirt is closely gored, and is carried up to form a corselet. Scarlet poplin corsage, dotted with large jet beads. Fancy muslin cap. *Fig. c.* Evening dress of arsenic green silk, trimmed with three puffings of white silk. The overskirt is white crepe, dotted with green and trimmed with quillings of green silk and a lace flounce. The corsage has a deep basque, trimmed with a lace flounce headed by a lace quilling. The sleeve is merely a puff of white silk, veiled by the lace bertha. The hair is worn in a puffed chignon, clasped by a fancy gilt comb. *Fig. d.* Walking costume of white poplin, trimmed with bias bands of mauve velvet and large velvet buttons. White felt hat, trimmed with mauve velvet, and mauve kid boots. *Fig. e.* Dinner dress of brown silk, trimmed with matching velvet and wide Cluny lace. The low corsage is worn with a high chemisette of Cluny, and puffs of thin muslin. The sleeves are a decided novelty, being of very great length, and caught together at the back of the waist. The coiffure is scarlet velvet, with pearl drops. *Fig. f.* Walking dress of purple reps, trimmed with bands of black velvet, studded with jet beads. The hem is cut in very sharp points, and displays a reps petticoat of a lighter shade. The sack is cut slightly to the figure at the back, and finished with deep points. Bonnet of bright green velvet.

PLATE 39. DECEMBER 1867. *Fig. a.* Visiting dress of green Irish poplin, trimmed with velvet bands, guipure lace, and jet ornaments. Bonnet of black velvet, with a fall of black lace. *Fig. b.* Evening dress of deep violet silk, trimmed on the edge of the skirt by a pinked, box-plaited ruffle with a silk band studded with large beads or buttons. The overdress is striped violet-and-white silk, trimmed with bands of violet silk studded with beads, and Cluny lace. The low, square corsage is filled in with a fluting of French muslin. The wreath is of violets with frosted foliage. *Fig. c.* Reception dress of Bismarck silk, with overskirt of black silk trimmed with narrow velvet and jet ornaments. The corsage is black silk, and the sleeves are Bismarck trimmed with gimp. Satin bonnet, with jet. *Fig. d.* Blue silk dinner dress with three full puffs and a pinked ruching of white silk at the hem. The overskirt is cut in deep scallops, finished with a row of lace. Pieces of black velvet trimmed with jet buttons extend down each gore of the upper skirt. The corsage is low and square, filled in by a fulling of white silk. *Fig. e.* Dinner dress of light magenta silk, with a very long train. The upper skirt is slashed and trimmed with velvet and a deep silk-and-chenille fringe. The corsage is cut low and square, and worn with a thin muslin chemisette edged with Cluny lace.

PLATE 40. JANUARY 1869. *Fig. a.* Purple velveteen walking suit with two skirts, the lower one just touching the ground, edged with a quilling of black satin. Upper skirt has apron front and pannier back, trimmed with fringe headed by satin bands. Pannier fastened with satin leaves. Tight jacket with sash. Velvet bonnet. *Fig. b.* Home dress of gray silk poplin, trimmed with four narrow folds scalloped and bound with green satin. The upper skirt is trimmed with a quilling of green satin, and looped up at each side with a rosette. The upper part of the skirt is trimmed with black lace and satin to simulate a basque, finished by a bow and long ends in back. Green satin belt, with fan-shaped bow in back. *Fig. c.* Walking dress of scarlet silk poplin, with an overdress of black velvet. White uncut velvet bonnet. *Fig. d.* Gray silk dinner dress. The front of the skirt is trimmed with three ruffles bound with blue. The left side is cut longer, lined with blue satin, and trimmed by the narrow ruffle which extends across the back. The dress is looped in three puffs by blue rosettes. The right side is lined with satin, turned back, edged with a narrow ruffle extending up the side. Low square corsage, a blue ruche edging. White muslin sleeves, puffed, with blue satin bands. *Fig. e.* Costume for a little boy, of black velvet trimmed with silk braid, with short Garibaldi pants and blouse. Scarlet stockings. High black boots. Black velvet hat, lined with scarlet. *Fig. f.* Walking suit of Havana brown cloth. The lower skirt is edged with a plaited quilling. The upper one is cut in points, edged with fancy gimp. Mantelet looped in the back and sides with a bow and rosettes. Cape looped in the back with a rosette and trimmed with fringe and narrow gimp.

PLATE 41. MARCH 1869. *Fig. a.* Green silk dress, trimmed with a row of knotted fringe and bias satin bands. Black velvet cloak without sleeves, trimmed with satin; satin belt and a large satin bow and ends in back. Green silk bonnet. *Fig. b.* Boy's suit of Havana brown cashmere, with pants and blouse. High boots of black kid. Straw hat. *Fig. c.* Dinner-dress of mauve silk. Underskirt is a lighter shade, trimmed with five narrow pinked ruffles; the upper skirt is cut in deep scallops, trimmed with ruffles. Low square corsage. Black lace cape, fastened by a satin bow. Hair heavily crimped, with a headdress of purple flowers and black lace. *Fig. d.* Walking dress of wine Irish poplin, with two skirts; the upper one puffed. Heavy black corded-silk cloak, trimmed with lace and satin pipings. Black felt hat. *Fig. e.* Watteau style evening dress. The underskirt is white silk, edged with a flounce headed with a plaited quilling. The upper dress is tulle, looped up with sprays of roses and leaves. The neck is finished with a wreath of flowers, which also forms the sleeves. Hair rolled and finished with a wreath of roses. *Fig. f.* Walking dress of black silk. The lower skirt is trimmed with three quillings of blue silk; the upper skirt forms a pannier in the back, looped up with silk bows. The front is cut in apron form, and is blue silk. Blue corsage and sleeves; small black silk cape. Bonnet of white uncut velvet.

PLATE 42. MAY 1869. *Fig. a.* Dress of cuir silk. The front is trimmed with narrow pinked ruffles with satin rosettes, arranged in scallops graduated to the waist. Low square corsage, trimmed to match. Puffed muslin waist, with lace insertions. *Fig. b.* Costume for a girl of eight years. Underskirt of scarlet cashmere cut in points, with a puffed tunic of black silk. Sacque of plain-colored cloth, trimmed to match the underskirt. White straw hat. *Fig. c.* Robe of white organdy, striped with blue with white flowers. The lower skirt and upper part of waist are plain blue; the underskirt is bordered by seven narrow ruffles. The upper skirt, shoulders, and center back are trimmed with looped ribbon bows with long ends. White silk parasol. *Fig. d.* Walking suit of black silk. The lower skirt is laid in plaits like a deep flounce with a puff, about three inches

from the ground. The upper skirt is cut up at the sides and trimmed to match. Paletot, in Watteau style, trimmed to match the skirt. Black lace bonnet. *Fig. e.* Dress of green silk; silk trim edged with narrow lace. Mantilla fichu of black lace, extending down the back to form an upper skirt; a sash of green ribbon is fastened low in back; a small bow of same at the waist. *Fig. f.* Foulard silk robe. Lilac silk underskirt, with one ruffle, headed by a quilling of silk. The upper skirt and waist are of white spotted with lilac, and looped up with lilac rosettes. Plain corsage, with small square cape trimmed with two ruffles. White chip bonnet.

PLATE 43. OCTOBER 1869. *Fig. a.* Dinner-dress of Metternich green silk. The skirt is trimmed with a row of fringe, headed by five narrow satin folds. High corsage; coat sleeve. Overdress of black lace, looped up with satin bows in back. *Fig. b.* Costume for a little girl. Underskirt of blue-and-gray striped satin. Gray poplin overskirt, blue trim. Low square corsage; white waist. White hat. *Fig. c.* Walking dress of purple silk. The hem is edged with a ruffle headed by a fluting, bands of satin fastened with buttons, and another fluting. Tight-fitting polonaise, forming an upper skirt in back, trimmed with satin and lace. The front is like a vest. White velvet bonnet. *Fig. d.* Walking suit of Havana brown. The dress is poplin, the skirt trimmed in the back with quillings fastened with rosettes. Plush cloak, tight-fitting, cut in points, and trimmed with satin. Brown velvet bonnet. *Fig. e.* Visiting dress of blue silk, with looped-up overskirt, trimmed with satin and white lace. Plain corsage, trimmed with satin and lace. White lace bonnet. *Fig. f.* Dress of pearl-colored poplin, trimmed with two narrow green fluted ruffles. The back of the skirt is formed of ruffles and puffs. Short jacket and front of dress trimmed with leaves of green velvet. Hat of white silk.

PLATE 44. APRIL 1872. *Fig. a.* Green silk dress, the skirt trimmed with one deep plaited ruffle; black silk overdress trimmed with a plaited silk ruffle. *Fig. b.* White cashmere dress for child of six, made with a basque waist, with cape cut in turrets and bound with pink silk. Bow and sash ends in back. White chip hat. *Fig. c.* Visiting dress of very light stone-colored silk, with overdress, waist, and sleeves of blue silk. The waist is cut in vest form, with a band of blue in front; the hem is trimmed with stone ruffles and squares of blue. Point appliqué lace bows and bands of blue silk with buttons trim the front of the skirt. Hat of stone-colored chip. *Fig. d.* Dress of nankeen silk pongee, with demi-train and polonaise; the skirt is trimmed with brown silk and fringe; the polonaise is trimmed with bands of silk fastened with buckles, and fringe. Open sleeves, trimmed to match. Hat of nankeen straw. *Fig. e.* Carriage dress of lilac silk, with demi-train. Trimmed with ruffles of two shades of silk, the ruffles deeper in back than in front and divided at the sides by a quilling and bows. Black silk polonaise, trimmed with white silk under black lace. Black lace hat. *Fig. f.* Evening dress of pink silk. The lower skirt is trimmed with puffs of white silk, divided by bands of pink silk lace and small bows; the overskirt is open in back, and trimmed with point appliqué lace. Low corsage, with jacket back, also trimmed with lace.

PLATE 45. JULY 1872. *Fig. a.* Dress of ecru batiste, with polonaise; the skirt trimmed with pieces of the material bound with a band of a darker shade. The polonaise is cut with a vest front and braided with a darker shade. White chip hat. *Fig. b.* Dress of light aqua silk grenadine, over silk of the same shade; the skirt has a plaited ruffle, with a puff and bows of black velvet. Polonaise of lace, striped with velvet. It is trimmed with white Valenciennes and black guipure lace. The silk waist is cut low and the overwaist surplice; long open sleeves. *Fig. c.* White piqué dress for a boy of three years; skirt and jacket trimmed with braid and buttons. White straw hat. *Fig. d.* Walking dress of dove gray silk, with a polonaise. The skirt, polonaise with a vest, and open sleeves are all trimmed with embroidery. Hat of black Neapolitan; black lace veil. *Fig. e.* Evening dress of white silk grenadine over white silk, and forming a court train. The dress is embroidered with birds and flowers in gay colors; white silk underskirt trimmed with ruffles and bands of lilac silk; the skirt revers are lilac silk. Basque waist cut square at the neck and trimmed to match. Hair in puffs with flowers and bird. *Fig. f.* Dinner dress of pink silk with a court train, the front trimmed with alternate ruffles of pink and black. Basque waist cut in a low square, with vest in front, trimmed with white lace and black silk; sleeves with two deep lace ruffles.

PLATE 46. NOVEMBER 1872. *Fig. a.* Evening dress of pink silk, trimmed with narrow silk ruffles; pink tulle overdress, looped up high on the sides. Low corsage, with silk bertha; flowers on shoulders and around bertha. Half wreath of flowers in hair. *Fig. b.* Green silk poplin kilt suit for boy of three years, with silk buttons up the front; black velvet sash tied in a large bow at the side. *Fig. c.* Evening dress of white silk with a court train, the front trimmed with plaited white and lilac ruffles. Lace apron, fastened at sides by bows of ribbon and flowers. Low basque corsage, trimmed with lilac silk and lace. *Fig. d.* Carriage dress of light bronze silk. Skirt trimmed with a deep ruffle, white lace, black lace, and velvet; black velvet polonaise, white and black lace trim. Velvet hat. *Fig. e.* Walking dress of dark blue silk, with apron front overskirt; the skirt has two ruffles trimmed with a narrow velvet border, extending up the back of skirt; overskirt trimmed to match. Blue velvet hat. *Fig. f.* Carriage dress of gray silk, with polonaise. The skirt has one ruffle with embroidered edge, finished by a band of bias silk at top; the polonaise has a basque in the back, open sleeves, and is trimmed with embroidery, which extends up the back. Bonnet of velvet.

PLATE 47. FEBRUARY 1873. *Fig. a.* Dinner dress; the lower skirt is lavender silk, trimmed with a pearl silk ruffle, with fringe and point appliqué lace. Polonaise is pearl-color with a lavender vest; it is trimmed with lace, fringe, and lavender bands. *Fig. b.* Dark blue velvet suit for boy of five years. Scarlet stockings; black felt hat, with scarlet wing. *Fig. c.* House dress of pale green silk, a court train with revers of a darker shade of velvet; the front is trimmed with a ruffle edged in pointed scallops, above a plaiting of velvet; a puff and velvet quillings head the ruffle. Basque waist, trimmed with lace and velvet revers and cuffs. *Fig. d.* Visiting dress of lilac silk; the front trimmed with narrow ruffles, silk bands of a darker shade, and bows of ribbon. Black silk polonaise, white silk revers. Violet velvet bonnet. *Fig. e.* Evening dress of white tarletane; the lower skirt trimmed with six puffs; the overskirt is trimmed with pink silk bands and a narrow ruffle at top and bottom; pink ribbon sash fastens at the side, and forms the looping of the overskirt in back. Basque waist cut surplice, and short sleeves match overskirt. *Fig. f.* Walking dress of two shades of brown; the lower skirt and waist are silk, the overskirt is cashmere. Velvet bonnet.

PLATE 48. MARCH 1873. *Fig. a.* Gray silk house dress, made with a polonaise; the skirt has a plaiting of the silk, headed by a band of brown silk and brown bows; a brown ruffle below. Polonaise is cut in points, bound with brown silk; the front of waist and skirt are brown silk; brown puffed sleeve. *Fig. b.* Dinner dress of black silk, with a long train; polonaise of cherry silk, scalloped, bound and edged with fringe. It is cut to show a black silk vest, has a basque in the back, and open sleeves. Hair arranged in puffs, with silver Marguerites. *Fig. c.* Evening dress of light blue silk. The lower skirt is trimmed with a ruffle of scalloped silk, headed by a flounce of black lace. Overskirt has an apron front, deep in the back, trimmed with lace, and a ruche of silk, pink roses, and foliage down the

sides. Basque waist cut low surplice; short sleeves; white muslin and lace on neck and arms; bouquets on shoulders and fastening dress in front. *Fig. d.* Evening dress of ecru silk, the skirt en tablier with lace inserting, and passementerie ornaments. Overskirt of black figured lace. Corsage cut low surplice; puffed sleeves, covered with net, and edged with lace. Pink roses and gold lace in hair. *Fig. e.* Visiting dress of two shades of lilac silk; the lower skirt trimmed with a ruffle; the overskirt and capes cut in points and embroidered. Bonnet of lilac silk.

PLATE 49. APRIL 1873. *Fig. a.* Walking dress of gray silk. The skirt is trimmed with four ruffles of brown silk, en tablier; the back is trimmed with brown ruffles; brown plaitings down each side. Plain corsage with open sleeves, sash in back, trimmed to match skirt. Bonnet of gray chip. *Fig. b.* Dress for child of four years, of pink cotton satine, trimmed with black braid, with high corsage, basque, tabs on the skirt falling from waist, and a small round cape and collar all trimmed with black braid and finished with a ruffle. Straw hat. *Fig. c.* Evening dress of blue silk; the lower skirt is trimmed with three plaited ruffles, the overskirt with point appliqué lace and ribbon bows of a darker shade than the dress. Low corsage; puffed elbow sleeves, trimmed with lace and ribbon. *Fig. d.* Walking dress of violet silk. Mantle of heavy black silk; silk and jet bead embroidery. Black bonnet. *Fig. e.* Bride's dress of thick white faille. The lower skirt is trimmed with two ruffles, a narrow one, box-plaited with pieces of the silk bound with satin between each plait; a wide flounce is over this. Overskirt and waist trimmed with fringe and satin piping. Basque waist, cut surplice, with lace at the neck. Open sleeves, with quilled lace around the hand. Tulle veil, and half-wreath of orange blossoms and buds. *Fig. f.* House dress of silk. The back of the skirt has ten narrow pale blue ruffles; the front and the waist are a lighter shade. The skirt front is trimmed with tucks of silk, in points. The sleeve ruffles and the vest are of the darker shade.

PLATE 50. JANUARY 1874. *Fig. a.* Dinner dress of crimson silk. The skirt is trimmed en tablier with a kilt plaiting, lace, and folds; the back, with quillings and shells made of silk, kilt plaits, and silk bows down the sides. Basque bodice, cut surplice, finished with a silk cord; sleeves with deep pointed cuff. Muslin fraise at the neck. *Fig. b.* Suit for little boy of four years. Black velvet, trimmed with fur. Matching boots and cap. *Fig. c.* Walking dress of purple silk and velvet. The lower skirt is silk, with a plaiting and two bands of silver fox fur. Velvet overskirt and mantle, also trimmed with fox. Light gray felt hat. *Fig. d.* Evening dress of light green silk with a deep pointed basquine. The lower skirt has a box-plaited ruffle cut in points at the top; the overskirt and waist are trimmed with Valenciennes lace and narrow folds of silk; wide sash looping up the back. *Fig. e.* Evening dress of pink and white silk. The underskirt is pink, with a ruffle of embroidered muslin, headed with a puff of French muslin and pink grosgrain ribbon loops and ends. The polonaise is trimmed with Valenciennes lace, looped up with pink flowers and ribbon; pink ribbon sash with fringed ends. *Fig. f.* Visiting dress of tea-colored silk, trimmed with quillings of velvet of a darker shade. The skirt is very long in the back, and is looped with a velvet sash; short apron front, velvet trim. Basque waist, trimmed with velvet, velvet vest, fraise at the neck and sleeve cuffs. Velvet bonnet.

PLATE 51. MAY 1874. *Fig. a.* Dinner dress of pink silk; the back of the skirt has one ruffle, the front is trimmed with ruffles and puffs. Deep basque waist and sleeves, trimmed with pleated ruffles. *Fig. b.* Reception dress of lilac silk, made with one skirt and polonaise trimmed with black lace, to simulate three skirts. The skirt is trimmed with one ruffle, plaited at intervals. Pieces of silk trimmed with black lace head this ruffle. The surplice neck has a fraise of white illusion. *Fig. c.* Carriage dress of two shades of green silk. The underskirt has a ruffle of the darker silk at the hem; the front and sides are trimmed with narrow ruffles of the light shade. The polonaise has a basque back, and is trimmed with revers of the light silk, dark buttons, and false buttonholes. Open sleeves, with narrow ruffles up the back of the arm. White chip bonnet. *Fig. d.* Walking dress of two shades of tea-colored silk and cashmere. The skirt front has broad kilt plaits of both shades; the back has narrow ruffles to the waist, finished by bows at the sides. Basque waist; open coat sleeves; sash on the right side. White chip bonnet. *Fig. e.* Evening dress of white silk; the skirt trimmed with one deep ruffle, headed with puffs of illusion. The overskirt and the top of puffs are trimmed with grapes and foliage. Pointed corsage, low neck, puff sleeve, and illusion puff around the neck. Hair in puffs and curls, with bunch of grapes and foliage.

PLATE 52. JULY 1874. *Fig. a.* House dress of bronze green grenadine. The waist is plaited into a square yoke, trimmed with a pointed one of silk, and forms a basque; plaited sleeves. Silk fraise at the neck, with feather trim. Chatelaine bag fastened at left side. *Fig. b.* Dress for child of three years, made of blue cashmere, with underwaist of white muslin. *Fig. c.* Walking dress of two shades of lilac silk. The underskirt is trimmed with tucks of silk divided by bands and bows of the darker; the overskirt is edged with a band of the darker with a narrow patterned braid. Sleeveless basque of the darker shade. Bonnet of silk and crepe. *Fig. d.* Evening dress of white French muslin and pink silk. The skirt is trimmed with five puffs of muslin, with a draped apron overskirt in front. The waist and partial court train are pink silk, trimmed with Valenciennes lace and pink silk cords. Hair in puffs and curls, with gold beads and pink feather. *Fig. e.* House dress of pale green silk, with deep basque waist; the back of the skirt has a deep plaiting with a puff and narrow ruffle of dark silk; the front is covered with puffs; the sides with bands of darker silk; waist and sleeves trimmed to match. *Fig. f.* Walking dress of black grenadine. The underskirt is trimmed with lengthwise puffs below a narrow plaited ruffle; the overskirt and basque waist are trimmed with guipure lace. Jacket of black silk, bound with galloon. Black lace capote.

PLATE 53. SEPTEMBER 1874. Fig. a. House dress of pale green silk. The underskirt is trimmed with a ruffle and puffs; the overskirt plaited in kilt plaits; the basque bodice is trimmed with folds of the silk. *Fig. b.* Suit of light brown cloth for boy of six years, trimmed with silk braid of a darker shade. Straw or felt hat, trimmed with brown velvet. *Fig. c.* Walking dress of violet silk and cashmere. The underskirt is silk, in lengthwise puffs; the polonaise is cashmere corded with silk; flaring collar with ruff of lace inside. Bonnet of straw. *Fig. d.* Evening dress of white silk, with tulle overdress trimmed with long garlands of roses and foliage; low bodice, with fraise of tulle around the neck. Flowers in hair match those on the dress. *Fig. e.* Visiting dress of two shades of blue silk. The underskirt and sleeves are light, trimmed with the dark; the polonaise is of the darker silk. Bonnet of both shades. *Fig. f.* Dinner dress of two shades of brown silk; the front is made of the darker shade; the rest of the dress is of the lighter silk; neck cut surplice with standing collar and muslin ruche.

PLATE 54. OCTOBER 1874. *Fig. a.* Visiting dress of purple silk and camel's hair. The underskirt is silk in lengthwise puffs, divided by bias bands corded; the coat is camel's hair, corded, and faced with silk. Bonnet of velvet and satin. *Fig. b.* Dress for child of four years, made of green silk poplin, cut gored, and trimmed with buttons and bands of velvet. Hat of matching velvet. *Fig. c.* Walking dress of two shades of brown silk and cashmere. The underskirt is of silk of the darker shade, with a

ruffle and puff, and standing ruffles; the polonaise is of cashmere of the lighter shade, with sleeves, sash, and fraise of the dark silk. Hat of grosgrain and velvet. *Fig. d.* Dinner dress of blue silk, with puff and ruffles in the back, and alternate ruffles of silk and lace in front; basque corsage, cut surplice; open sleeves, trimmed with lace. *Fig. e.* Evening dress of pink and white silk and lace. The long train and bodice are pink; the revers at sides are lined with white, trimmed with lace and bouquets of pink roses. Lace fraise around the low neck, and trimming the corsage to form a short basque. *Fig. f.* Evening dress, suitable for a bridesmaid, of white silk and illusion. Silk underskirt, trimmed with a kilt plaiting, headed with Valenciennes lace. Overdress of illusion, looped up with grapes and foliage; the corsage has a low neck, with deep basques trimmed with lace; ribbon bow on the shoulders. Hair arranged in finger puffs, with wreath of grapes and foliage.

PLATE 55. NOVEMBER 1874. *Fig. a.* House dress of two shades of green silk. The underskirt is made of kilt plaits of both colors; the front of the overskirt is formed of puffs divided by bows of both shades; the back has folds of the two. Bodice of the lighter shade with sleeves of the darker. *Fig. b.* Dress for boy of three years; blue cashmere, trimmed with white braid and buttons. *Fig. c.* Walking dress of dark brown silk with overdress and sacque of camel's hair of a lighter shade, fastened by ribbon bows in front and on the sleeves. Felt hat. Black marten boa and muff. *Fig. d.* Visiting dress of claret satin and velvet. The underskirt is of quilted satin; overdress and basque bodice are velvet, trimmed with satin. Bonnet of matching velvet. *Fig. e.* Dinner dress of violet silk. The front and sides of the skirt are covered with lengthwise puffs divided by narrow gathered ruffles. Basque surplice bodice and sleeves trimmed with narrow ruffles gathered at the top. *Fig. f.* Evening dress of white silk, the skirt trimmed with three ruffles headed with a garland of roses and leaves. Low, square-pointed corsage, with illusion laid in plaits over the neck; the dress edged with flowers; puff sleeves.

PLATE 56. MAY 1875. *Fig. a.* Dress of light ecru batiste; the skirt formed of lengthwise puffs smaller in the back than the front. Puffs around the arm; brown silk cuffs and sleeveless double-breasted jacket. Ecru chip bonnet. *Fig. b.* House dress of gray silk, the front trimmed with puffs and plaitings, finished at the sides with bows. The back has one puff, a plaiting, and a long overskirt. Blue silk body, trimmed with cord and ornaments. *Fig. c.* Evening dress of white and pink silk. Underskirt of white, trimmed up the front and on the back with narrow lengthwise ruffles and pink ruches. Low basque bodice and overskirt of pink silk, trimmed with white lace and black velvet. *Fig. d.* Dinner dress of green silk. The front of the skirt made in kilt plaits, with bands of darker green silk crossing it, with ornaments at the ends. The back is ruffled to the waist. The sides and the sleeves are trimmed with the darker silk. Sleeveless basque of black lace over plain cuirass bodice. *Fig. e.* House dress of lilac silk, trimmed with ruffles. Overskirt at the sides and back. Cuirass basque, cut surplice, with standing white muslin ruff. Sleeves slightly open, made of lengthwise puffs.

PLATE 57. JUNE 1875. *Fig. a.* Walking dress of two shades of brown silk. The front of the skirt made in kilt plaits. Apron overskirt and sash of the darker shade. Basque bodice, dark silk trim. Chip hat. *Fig. b.* Evening dress of two shades of blue silk. The front of the skirt is made of diamonds of the darker, with the lighter silk between them, plaiting at the sides. Low corsage, buttoned up the front, with lace at the neck. Hair in finger puffs, with twisted strings of pearls. *Fig. c.* Visiting dress of two shades of purple. The front is made of puffs and plaitings of light on dark; the sides have pieces of dark buttoned over; the back is trimmed with a plaited ruffle, the upper part arranged in a pouf. Basque bodice of the dark, with trim and sleeves of the light. Bonnet of both shades. *Fig. d.* Dress for girl of six, of gray summer cashmere trimmed with pink silk. The skirt is trimmed with two ruffles. Basque bodice and sash. Gray chip hat. *Fig. e.* Dinner dress of green silk. The front of the skirt trimmed with puffs and white lace; the sides and back are plaited, the sides and the bodice trimmed with bands of velvet and velvet bows. Basque bodice, surplice neck, trimmed with lace and velvet. *Fig. f.* Evening dress of white muslin over pink silk. Silk underskirt is trimmed with a plaiting. Long muslin apron overskirt, and trained skirt, trimmed with Mechlin lace, a thick roll of muslin banded with pink ribbon and garlands of flowers. Low corsage, pink silk in front, plaited white muslin in back, trimmed with lace; short sleeves.

PLATE 58. OCTOBER 1875. *Fig. a.* Visiting dress of pale lavender. The underskirt is silk, the back plaited, the front in folds and puffed. Polonaise mantle of silk warp cashmere of a darker shade, embroidered and trimmed with fringe. Silk bonnet. *Fig. b.* House dress of two shades of green silk, the skirt in kilt plaits in both colors. Basque bodice, with a piece of the lighter silk plaited down the back which falls over the skirt, forming a pouf and sash ends. *Fig. c.* Evening dress of pink silk; the front of skirt is trimmed with ruffles, the back plaited with bows down the center. Low corsage, trimmed with white lace. Overdress made of a white lace shawl. *Fig. d.* Dinner dress of silver gray silk; the front covered with lengthwise puffs of blue silk. Low corsage, with pieces falling from it down the skirt, trimmed with blue silk and fringe. Hair arranged in a catagon braid, fastened with flowers in small bouquets. *Fig. e.* Walking dress of plum and ecru silk. The front is kilt-plaited from waist to hem; the back is trimmed with narrow ruffles. The overskirt is fastened into the sides and is knotted in the back. Basque bodice with ecru kerchief and cuffs. Bonnet of silk and velvet.

PLATE 59. SEPTEMBER 1875. *Fig. a.* Carriage dress of dark blue silk with trimming of a lighter blue. The underskirt is trimmed with folds and knife-plaited ruffles. The overskirt is trimmed with knife plaiting. The bodice is cut surplice, and trimmed to match the underskirt. Silk bonnet. *Fig. b.* Pink silk evening dress. The underskirt is trimmed with lace, bouquets of roses, and puffs. Overskirt only in the back, and trimmed with lace and flowers. Pointed low-necked bodice and elbow sleeves, trimmed with lace; the kerchief at the neck is crepe lisse. *Fig. c.* Walking dress of purple silk, the skirt made with a pouf in the back with sash and ruffles of black. Black sleeveless jacket, lace and passementerie trim; purple sleeves, black cuffs. Black lace bonnet. *Fig. d.* Walking dress of black silk. The upper skirt is trimmed with jet fringe in front only, and two rows of buttons down the right side. The back is in plaits, the sides are trimmed with ruffles and puffs. Basque bodice and coat sleeves, trimmed with jet. Black chip bonnet.

PLATE 60. JANUARY 1876. *Fig. a.* Carriage dress of two shades of green silk and velvet; the underskirt is silk, the front is trimmed with a ruffle headed with puffs of velvet; a broad plait down the back has a pouf at the top. The overskirt is velvet and silk, trimmed with fringe; velvet bodice, long in front, short in back, piped with silk. Velvet bonnet. *Fig. b.* Walking dress of elephant gray silk and plaid camel's hair; the underskirt is silk, trimmed with plaitings. The overskirt is plaid, with silk plaitings. Cuirass bodice of silk, with plaid sleeves, silk pocket. Velvet bonnet. *Fig. c.* Dinner dress of lilac silk, the skirt trimmed with a plaiting; overskirt and trimming of black thread lace, with velvet sash in back. Hair in puffs, with a cluster of pink roses fastening a Spanish veil of black lace. *Fig. d.* Evening dress of pink silk, skirt and muslin overskirt trimmed with a plaiting of white French muslin, headed with a Valenciennes insertion. Cuirass bodice, muslin sleeves. *Fig. e.* Visiting dress of blue silk, the skirt trimmed with narrow ruf-

fles and a plaiting. Overdress and cuirass basque of dark blue velvet matelassé; plain velvet sleeves. Velvet bonnet.

PLATE 61. MAY 1876. *Fig. a.* Evening dress of pink silk; the back cut with a long train and a pouf at the top. The front is trimmed entirely with knife plaitings; the back with one. The bodice and sash overskirt, which fastens in a bow in the back, are of white matelassé, trimmed with a netted fringe. The sleeves are trimmed with two rows of lace. *Fig. b.* House dress of blue silk and plaid camel's hair. The underskirt is trimmed with ruffles; the bodice and overskirt button down the back, and fasten with a bow. Coat sleeves, buttoned down the outside of the arm. *Fig. c.* Dinner dress of lilac silk and matelassé. The underskirt is plain silk, with ruffles and scarf drapery of the matelassé. Cuirass basque with vest and sleeves of plain silk. *Fig. d.* Costume for child of four years, made of blue cashmere. Hat of chip, trimmed with ribbon to match dress. *Fig. e.* Reception dress of green silk and grenadine. The underskirt and bodice are silk; the overdress (which fastens under the arms) is of figured silk grenadine, trimmed with narrow silk pipings. Silver chatelaine encircles the waist. Silver Marguerites in the hair. *Fig. f.* Walking dress of coffee camel's hair. The underskirt is trimmed with two knife plaitings headed with bias bands of plaid. The overskirt consists of two aprons; the lower one plain, bound with stripes; the upper one striped. Sacque bodice to match overskirt, with plain vest and sleeves. Brown straw bonnet.

PLATE 62. JULY 1876. *Fig. a.* House dress of elephant gray silk and grenadine. The lower skirt is silk, front and sides kilt plaited, the back plain. The scarf drapery forming the overskirt is grenadine, trimmed with fringe, ribbon bows at the sides. Basque waist of grenadine with kilt plaits in back. *Fig. b.* Evening dress of pink silk. The underskirt is trimmed with plaitings on the front, plain train. Polonaise of India muslin; low neck, trimmed with garlands of roses and foliage and puffs and Valenciennes lace. Bertha of lace and flowers; pink ribbon sash. *Fig. c.* Afternoon dress of blue damask and silk. The underskirt and sleeves are damask; the overdress and basque are silk, with a band of darker blue and fringe. *Fig. d.* Walking dress of pale green silk. The upper part cut as a polonaise, the skirt kilted under the sash; black silk sleeves and trimming. Black chip bonnet. *Fig. e.* Walking dress of purple silk and lilac plaid grenadine. The underskirt is silk, trimmed with knife plaiting and puff. The overskirt and basque are grenadine, trimmed with a knife plaiting of silk; silk sleeves. Lilac chip bonnet.

PLATE 63. AUGUST 1876. *Fig. a.* Walking dress of navy blue silk with two skirts, both trimmed with plaid grenadine in two shades of blue. The basque is grenadine, with silk sleeves. Bonnet of blue silk and crepe. *Fig. b.* Bride's dress of white silk. Overskirt trimmed in front with fringe and garlands of orange blossoms, the sides with plaitings; the back with puffs of illusion and plaitings of Valenciennes lace. Basque bodice, trimmed with fringe. Illusion veil; half wreath of orange blossoms. *Fig. c.* Walking dress of purple grenadine and silk of two shades. The skirt is grenadine with silk trimming and pocket. Basque bodice of grenadine, with silk sleeves. White chip bonnet. *Fig. d.* Visiting dress of matelassé and brown silk. The underskirt is silk, the polonaise is matelassé, buttoned at the side. Brown sash. Pearl-colored chip bonnet. *Fig. e.* Carriage dress of two shades of green silk. The back of the skirt is dark, trimmed with a plaiting and ruffle. The overskirt is the light shade, which is striped; fringed trim. Basque bodice of plain green, with striped sleeves. Crepe de Chine bonnet.

PLATE 64. OCTOBER 1876. *Fig. a.* Evening dress of pink silk, with box-plaited flounce at hem. Low-necked polonaise, with puffed skirt of white gauze, trimmed with lace and pink flowers; pink ribbon sash. Pink silk trimming and bow in back.

Fig. b. Walking dress of brown silk. The back is made with shirred puffs trimmed with lace; apron overskirt has openings at the sides, laced with narrow bands of silk. Basque bodice to match. Velvet bonnet. *Fig. c.* Carriage dress of two shades of purple silk. The underskirt and sash are dark, the polonaise light, with dark trim. Velvet bonnet. *Fig. d.* Walking dress of myrtle green silk and plaid camel's hair. The underskirt is silk, with narrow ruffles. The overskirt and basque are camel's hair, trimmed with fringe; silk sleeves. Silk bonnet. *Fig. e.* Walking dress of navy blue silk, with a polonaise and underskirt; the polonaise buttons down the back; the knife plaitings and ruffles are faced with cardinal red. Navy blue bonnet.

PLATE 65. NOVEMBER 1876. *Fig. a.* Dinner dress of violet silk and matelassé. The underskirt is silk, trimmed with a plaiting and puff; the overdress has a court train; apron front, trimmed with fringe, passing over the back, fastened by a bow. Basque bodice, elbow sleeves. *Fig. b.* Walking dress of elephant wool damassé. The underskirt is trimmed with a wide bias band of plaid silk, edged with narrow plaitings. The polonaise is trimmed with the plaid, and fringe. Velvet bonnet. *Fig. c.* Walking dress of light brown silk and matelassé, the underskirt of silk. Polonaise of matelassé, made very long, and trimmed with bands of Oriental embroidery and fringe, waist trimmed to match. Matching velvet bonnet. *Fig. d.* House dress of blue silk; plain underskirt, the polonaise buttoning over to one side, and trimmed with narrow braid forming stripes and a knotted fringe; pocket on left side. *Fig. e.* Evening dress of white illusion, with train of figured silk gathered in puffs and fastened with clusters of flowers. Pink silk corset waist; low neck, with bertha and sleeves of illusion.

PLATE 66. JANUARY 1877. *Fig. a.* Carriage dress of myrtle green silk and matelassé. Silk underskirt with a ruffle of matelassé with velvet bands. The long sacque is of the same, trimmed with velvet and braid. Velvet bonnet. *Fig. b.* Evening dress of blue silk. The skirt trimmed with a white gauze ruffle and a silk one; overskirt and drapery of white gauze edged with lace and looped with flowers. Low corsage, short sleeves, gauze bertha. *Fig. c.* Walking dress of purple velvet and striped damassé. The underskirt, sleeves, and trimming are velvet; the rest is damassé. Velvet pocket attached to belt. Silk bonnet. *Fig. d.* Dinner dress of pale gray silk and matelassé and pink silk. The skirt is trimmed with knife plaitings of gray, with the upper part of pink, a gray silk band, and small pink tassels. The back of the skirt and the bodice are matelassé and pink silk. *Fig. e.* Walking dress of elephant gray silk and camel's hair in two shades. The underskirt, sleeves, and trim are silk; the polonaise of camel's hair, trimmed with fringe. Velvet bonnet.

PLATE 67. FEBRUARY 1877. *Fig. a.* Walking dress of elephant gray silk and striped camel's hair, trimmed with fringe and velvet. Velvet bonnet. *Fig. b.* Sailor costume for boy of four years, made of navy blue cloth. Navy felt hat. *Fig. c.* Dinner dress of lilac silk, trimmed with white lace and silk. Surplice bodice, elbow sleeves. *Fig. d.* Walking dress of myrtle green cloth. The underskirt is trimmed with silk; the polonaise is cloth, trimmed with ball fringe. Velvet bonnet. *Fig. e.* Dinner or evening dress, of pale gray silk matelassé. The skirt front is pink silk, trimmed with gray fringe, with a deep netted heading of pink, and large pink silk bows; deep matelassé basque, trimmed with fringe; pink sleeves. *Fig. f.* Walking dress of plain brown silk, and striped camel's hair of a lighter shade. The skirt front and basque are camel's hair, trimmed with silk and buttons. Bonnet of silk and velvet.

PLATE 68. MARCH 1877. *Fig. a.* Evening dress of pink silk, with white feather edging. The underskirt is plain; the polonaise fastens slantwise, and is trimmed with a netted fringe headed with a band of feathers. *Fig. b.* Walking dress of two shades of brown silk, with polonaise. The underskirt is trimmed with one ruffle, edged with a narrow plaiting; the polonaise and sleeves with lace headed with velvet. Brown velvet bonnet and muff. *Fig. c.* Carriage dress of purple velvet with polonaise, trimmed with cords and ornaments, and a band of chinchilla fur. Purple velvet bonnet. Chinchilla fur muff. *Fig. d.* Gray cashmere dress for boy of three years, trimmed with cardinal silk and buttons. *Fig. e.* House dress of navy blue silk and gray matelassé. The underskirt is silk, trimmed with narrow ruffles and plaiting; the polonaise is gray, with blue silk sleeves and trim under the arms and down the skirt of the polonaise. *Fig. f.* House dress of myrtle green silk in princess shape, trimmed with narrow plaiting. Scarf overskirt, trimmed to match the dress.

PLATE 69. JUNE 1877. *Fig. a.* Visiting dress of two shades of gray silk. The dress and sacque are of the darker shade; the revers, plaiting, and trimming are of the light; revers and vest are trimmed with embroidery. Chip bonnet. *Fig. b.* Walking dress of two shades of purple silk; the skirt of the darker, trimmed with ruffles; polonaise of figured silk of a lighter shade, trimmed with purple fringe and ribbon; purple sleeves. Bonnet of lilac chip. *Fig. c.* Dinner dress of pearl gray grenadine; it is made with one skirt trimmed to simulate two, with a narrow ruffle of silk, white lace, and cardinal scarf. Cuirass basque with heart-shaped neck and elbow sleeves, trimmed with lace and cardinal silk. *Fig. d.* Evening dress of pale blue silk and damask, trimmed with white lace, narrow plaitings, and folds of the damask; basque bodice cut long in back, low neck. Damask and lace bertha. *Fig. e.* Evening dress of pink silk, the skirt front in crosswise plaits; the back long, trimmed with three rows of white lace and gathered to form a puff, fastened by a spray of flowers and leaves. Basque bodice, low neck; bertha with lace edging; bouquet of flowers on shoulder.

PLATE 70. SEPTEMBER 1877. *Fig. a.* Breton dress in two shades of green; the underskirt is silk, the overdress and jacket are cashmere, trimmed with embroidered braid and sequin buttons. *Fig. b.* Evening dress of pink silk, the skirt trimmed with a narrow plaited ruffle and a scarf drapery of white matelassé, trimmed with fringe and looped with flowers. Cuirass bodice, cut surplice, white collar and cuffs; elbow sleeves. *Fig. c.* Bride's dress of white silk, in Princess shape, buttoned slantwise, cut in turrets, as is the hem, both edged with narrow Valenciennes lace; small bouquets of orange blossoms fasten the dress; illusion veil, half wreath. *Fig. d.* Evening dress of two shades of lilac silk; the back cut like a court train and trimmed with white lace; basque bodice and elbow sleeves, trimmed with lace. *Fig. e.* Walking dress of two shades of brown camel's hair. Plain underskirt, with a brown ruffle and a plaid one; plaid overdress and basque, trimmed with plain fabric and buttons. Brown straw hat.

PLATE 71. MARCH 1878. *Fig. a.* Evening dress of pale blue silk, the skirt trimmed with a puff and narrow ruffles at the hem. The front has pieces trimmed with lace and gathered with roses extending from the top of corsage down the skirt. The basque corsage has low neck and short sleeves. *Fig. b.* Bride's dress of plain white silk; Princess back, basque front, and apron overskirt, cut in turrets and trimmed with a plaiting and orange blossoms. The dress is cut surplice with crepe lisse in the neck. Illusion veil and orange blossoms. *Fig. c.* Visiting dress of two shades of myrtle green velvet and damask. The underskirt and sleeves are velvet, the polonaise is damask, trimmed with fringe. Deep lace collar and cuffs. Bonnet of velvet and silk. *Fig. d.* Carriage dress of plum velvet and silk. The front of the skirt and waist and the sleeves are striped velvet and silk; the revers are plain silk, and the rest of the dress is velvet trimmed with embroidered bands of silk. Matching velvet and silk bonnet. *Fig. e.* Walking dress of elephant gray silk and wool damassé. The underskirt and sleeves are silk, the polonaise damassé. Silk bonnet.

PLATE 72. APRIL 1878. *Fig. a.* Walking dress of olive green silk and damassé. The dress is silk, with underskirt trimmed with a damassé band; the overdress is trimmed with damassé plaiting, bows, and a broad band from waist to hem making the overskirt fit tightly in front. Basque bodice, with sleeves and vest of damassé. Straw hat. *Fig. b.* House dress of plain purple silk, and striped silk bourrette. The skirt is striped, with scarf drapery of the plain. Deep basque, with vest of bourrette with turned-over collar cut surplice. *Fig. c.* Dinner dress of blue silk, with overdress and basque waist of striped grenadine, trimmed with ecru lace. Square-necked bodice, blue silk trim and sleeves. *Fig. d.* Evening dress of striped pink-and-white silk, trimmed with folds of plain pink silk and white Valenciennes lace. The basque is deep in front, buttoned off center, surplice neck with turned-over collar. *Fig. e.* House dress of brown silk and striped wool bourrette. The underskirt is trimmed with a puff and ruffle of brown silk in front, a band in the back, piped with color. The overskirt is silk, and striped, with colored fringe trim. Basque bodice, silk sleeves, silk and fringe trim.

PLATE 73. JULY 1878. *Fig. a.* Walking dress of two shades of moss green in Princess shape. The dress is grenadine in the light shade; the darker shade is silk, used for a scarf across the front, yoke, and sleeves. Straw bonnet. *Fig. b.* House dress of two shades of lilac silk. The front is dark, the sleeves and the back, shirred at intervals from neck to hem, are light; it is fastened at the sides with silk bows. *Fig. c.* Carriage dress of navy blue silk. The underskirt is trimmed with knife plaitings, the top one edged with white and black lace. The polonaise is trimmed with lace, with ecru ribbon bows and lace down the back and front. Bonnet of navy blue chip. *Fig. d.* Dinner dress of two shades of blue silk and grenadine, in Princess shape, cut surplice at the throat and trimmed with lace and ribbon bows. The skirt is trimmed with plaitings of silk and grenadine, and lace to match bodice and sleeves. Scarf drapery of grenadine, with bows of lace and ribbon fastening the sides. *Fig. e.* Evening dress of white silk grenadine damassé and plain pink silk, in Princess shape. The dress front is silk, with trimming of grenadine, pink fringe, and bands of silk. The back is trimmed with revers of silk and fringe. Low corsage, short sleeves.

PLATE 74. FEBRUARY 1879. *Fig. a.* Walking dress of plaid navy blue-and-gray cloth, with two skirts and yoke bodice. The underskirt is trimmed with a kilting, revers, and ribbon bows. Navy blue felt hat. *Fig. b.* Suit for boy of four years. Gray camel's hair, trimmed with cardinal silk bands and buttons. Gray felt hat, velvet trim. *Fig. c.* Visiting dress of seal brown silk, and brown striped satin and velvet, fringed trimming. Velvet and satin bonnet. *Fig. d.* Evening dress of pink silk, white silk, and white lace, in Princess shape, open in front over an underskirt. It is trimmed like a court train with plaitings of duchess lace separated by loops of pink and white satin ribbon. Square neck, duchess lace sleeves. Three vests of alternate white and pink silk fall below the waist over the underskirt. *Fig. e.* Dinner dress of blue damassé, trimmed with plain silk, cut in Princess shape halfway down the skirt, from which the front is laid in folds, and the back has pannier drapery. The front is cut in diamonds, with a plain silk plaiting underneath, and ribbon bows; slightly low neck with lace quilling, silk sleeves. *Fig. f.* Walking dress of two shades of green camel's hair, trimmed with plaitings. The front of the overskirt has a broad panel ornamented with rows of stitching. Jacket with vest. Green velvet bonnet.

PLATE 75. MARCH 1879. *Fig. a.* Highland costume for boy of four years, of green-and-blue plaid cloth trimmed with velvet.

Velvet cap, plaid stockings to match suit. *Fig. b.* House dress of cream-colored camel's hair, with moss green silk underskirt trimmed with narrow-plaited ruffles. The overskirt is pleated across the front and lengthwise in the back; pleated basque bodice. *Fig. c.* Evening dress of pink silk and white damask. The front is pink silk forming pleated scarfs trimmed with white chenille fringe; the back is white damask; pink silk sleeves. *Fig. d.* Walking dress of brown cashmere, the overskirt is open in points at the sides, with striped velvet and satin between; the vest is the same material. Ribbon bows on the front of overskirt. Brown felt hat. *Fig. e.* Dinner dress of two shades of blue silk and gauze. The front is kilt plaited, the polonaise is striped gauze, the edge cut in turrets and finished with lace, the revers faced with the darker silk; ribbon bows. *Fig. f.* Walking dress of two shades of deep gray silk and brocade. The back of the skirt is plain silk, the front is brocade with silk plaitings finished by ribbon bows; brocade jacket with plain silk vest. White felt bonnet.

PLATE 76. JUNE 1879. *Fig. a.* Pink silk evening dress with a long train, trimmed with white gauze ruffles. Striped gauze low-necked basque, with bertha of lace and flowers. Flowers trim skirt and left side of basque. *Fig. b.* Walking dress of sage silk trimmed with sage damassé; jacket bodice with surplice neck, damassé collar. Sage chip bonnet. *Fig. c.* Green camel's hair walking dress for three-year-old child; the back pleated, the front gored. Matching straw hat. *Fig. d.* Dinner dress of sapphire blue silk and gauze. The skirt is gauze, the front covered with narrow ruffles, scarf drapery of silk, and pleating across the back. Back of basque is silk trimmed with Breton lace, the front is gauze with ribbon lacing. *Fig. e.* Carriage dress of two shades of gray silk. Kilted underskirt and front of overskirt are dark gray; pleated basque and back of skirt are light gray. Chip bonnet. *Fig. f.* Lilac-and-purple striped grenadine reception dress, with plain purple ruffles, sleeves, and trim. Fringe trim on skirt and around hem of basque bodice.

PLATE 77. NOVEMBER 1879. *Fig. a.* Walking-dress of two shades of blue silk and cashmere. Kilted underskirt; overskirt cut square in front, looped up and turned back at the side, blue silk facing. Jacket waist, with plain silk vest; revers, cuffs, and pockets of damask. Velvet bonnet. *Fig. b.* Evening dress of plain pink silk and white satin brocaded with pink bouquets. The front of the skirt is silk, the bodice and back of the dress of the satin, the hem in back trimmed with band and pleating of pink and looped with bows of pink ribbon. Quilled Breton lace trim on corsage, extending down the skirt, increasing in width as it descends. *Fig. c.* Suit for boy of four years; peacock blue velvet jacket blouse and pants, inner vest of white cloth, collar and cuffs of the same. Scotch cap. *Fig. d.* Walking-dress of striped pekin in two shades of steel and plain satin; the underskirt is satin, trimmed with bias bands of the pekin; the overdress trimmed with the same. Dolman of camel's hair of a darker shade, lined with satin and trimmed with satin, passementerie, and fringe. Felt hat. *Fig. e.* House dress of green silk and plaid cheviot of ecru, with gay colors. The underskirt is silk, with one box-pleated ruffle. The polonaise has a short pannier, and scarf in pleats across the front of the skirt, fastened with a large bow at the right side. It is caught up with a large bunch of embroidered ribbon loops, and the vest is the same ribbon and green silk. *Fig. f.* Carriage dress and muff of purple velvet, with satin trim of a lighter shade. The underskirt is trimmed with pleated ruffles; the overskirt is slightly draped. Deep jacket with satin lining and cuffs. Muff edged with silver fox fur. Bonnet of twilled silk.

PLATE 78. OCTOBER 1880. *Fig. a.* Carriage dress of fawn-colored silk and cashmere. The underskirt is silk in lengthwise puffs, with narrow ruffles at the hem. The overdress and jacket are cashmere, edged with a band of embroidered satin; the overskirt is looped at the side with cord and tassels. Slightly open neck, with a matching plaited half handkerchief trimming. Silk bonnet. *Fig. b.* Evening dress of pink silk and white damassé, the front of underskirt is trimmed with puffs, under long tabs of damassé fastened with small bouquets of roses; the back is trimmed with alternate ruffles of white and pink. The overskirt is pink gauze, looped up with trailing sprays of roses. Basque bodice of white damassé, low neck trimmed with lace, silk, and roses. Pink roses in hair, fan of black lace and pink silk. *Fig. c.* Suit for child of five years. Garnet cashmere dress, striped velvet coat with vest, cuffs, and pocket of white damassé. Garnet velvet hat with pompon. *Fig. d.* Walking dress of two shades of purple, the darker shade of striped velvet and satin, the lighter damassé. The underskirt is striped, with a striped ruffle and quilling of light silk; the overdress is striped, with a second overdress forming a long pointed damassé apron. Deep jacket bodice with crosswise stripes, trimmed with damassé. Plain silk plaitings down the front. Bonnet of purple velvet. *Fig. e.* Walking dress of navy blue cloth. Kilted underskirt, overdress cut in long points, which cross and leave it open in front; it is stitched with cardinal silk, and looped with bows of the same color. Jacket bodice of tucks, with deep points in front, and cardinal silk vest. Navy blue felt bonnet. *Fig. f.* Walking dress of peacock green camel's hair. Underskirt trimmed with silk ruffles at hem, overskirt is shirred in front and trimmed with striped satin revers, and satin ribbon bow with spikes on the ends. Jacket bodice with striped satin vest, pockets, collar, and cuffs; these also have bows ornamented with spikes. Hat of matching velvet.

PLATE 79. NOVEMBER 1880. *Fig. a.* Walking dress of black cashmere. The underskirt has a box-plaited ruffle, the upper one is shirred, piped with cardinal silk, and cardinal ribbon bows. Cloak of black armure silk trimmed with fringe and passementerie. Black plush bonnet. *Fig. b.* Walking dress of purple damassé trimmed with darker plain goods; the dress is gathered with shirrings of the plain goods below the turrets of cuirass basque. Trimming on underskirt and back of overdress is of the darker shade. Plush and satin bonnet. *Fig. c.* Dress for child of six years, of peacock green cashmere trimmed with satin. White fur felt bonnet with peacock satin. *Fig. d.* Visiting dress of dark gray satin and cisele velvet in cashmere colors. The front drapery of the skirt is velvet, the back is also draped

with it, and the ruffles trimming hem faced and piped with it. It has a deep coat bodice, with cuffs, collar, pockets, and trimming of the velvet. Satin bonnet. *Fig. e.* Evening dress of ecru silk. Back of skirt is trimmed with narrow ruffles, the front with two narrow ruffles divided by a lace one, and deep vine embroidered in colors. Above these is a short scarf apron edged with lace. Square-necked basque, with elbow sleeves. Scarlet pomegranates trim neck of dress, and hair. *Fig. f.* Walking dress of dark brown cloth with a long polonaise. Front of underskirt is kilted under long tabs of cloth bound with satin. Back of skirt is trimmed with a box-pleated ruffle. Satin, cuffs, collar, pockets, and piping. Brown fur hat.

PLATE 80. DECEMBER 1880. *Fig. a.* Visiting dress of two shades of purple. Front of underskirt is composed of alternate puffs of both materials; the back is trimmed with two pleatings headed with a puff. The overskirt is the lighter shade satin damassé trimmed with fringe. Jacket of plush of the darker, with cuffs, pockets, and collar of the damassé. Bonnet of plush. *Fig. b.* House dress of two shades of blue. The underskirt is silk in the darker shade, kilted. Polonaise is wool damassé of the lighter shade, turned up in front with ribbon bows at the sides. Silk cuffs and sailor collar fastened with ribbon bow. *Fig. c.* Dress for child of five years, of brown plush and ecru camel's hair. The underskirt is plush, the jacket and scarf drapery on the skirt are camel's hair trimmed with fur. Ecru felt bonnet trimmed with brown plush. *Fig. d.* Evening dress of plain pink silk and striped satin. The underskirt is silk with a pleating headed with fans of lace and pleated silk. The front is striped satin, with scarf drapery fastened with bouquets of flowers. Short apron overskirt trimmed with duchess lace. Basque bodice, low square neck, striped vest, and white lace trim; bouquet of flowers on left side, flowers in hair to match those on skirt. *Fig. e.* Dinner dress of grenadine green silk. The underskirt is trimmed with two narrow pleatings, and both skirts have an embroidered white satin flounce. Basque bodice and elbow sleeves, trimmed with embroidered ruffles. Roses at the left side of the square neck. *Fig. f.* Walking dress of two shades of elephant silk and camel's hair. The plaited underskirt is silk; the scarf drapery on the skirt is figured camel's hair, fastened by a bow in front. The smock wrap is plain camel's hair, with gathered yoke and sleeves, trimmed with lace and ribbon bows. Plush bonnet.

PLATE 1. MAY 1841

PLATE 2. FEBRUARY 1838 AND JULY 1838

PLATE 3. NOVEMBER 1838 AND AUGUST 1838

a

b

c

d

PLATE 4. APRIL 1840

PLATE 5. SEPTEMBER 1840

a   *b*   *c*   *d*

PLATE 6. DECEMBER 1840

a   b   c   d

PLATE 7. FEBRUARY 1841

PLATE 8. JUNE 1841

a   b   c   d

PLATE 9. SEPTEMBER 1841

a   *b*   *c*   *d*

PLATE 10. MARCH 1842

a   b   c   d

PLATE 11. MAY 1842

a   b   c   d

PLATE 12. FEBRUARY 1843

a   b   c   d   e

PLATE 13. MARCH 1843

F. Humphreys. f.

a   b   c   d

PLATE 14. JULY 1843

PLATE 15. JANUARY 1843

a   b   c   d   e

PLATE 16. NOVEMBER 1843

a   b   c   d

Plate 17. January 1844

PLATE 18. MARCH 1844

a   b   c   d

Plate 19. 1845

a   b   c   d   e

PLATE 20. OCTOBER 1845

PLATE 21. APRIL 1845

PLATE 22. APRIL 1850 AND DECEMBER 1850

a

b

c

d

PLATE 25. OCTOBER 1858

a   b   c   d

a   b   c   d   e

PLATE 26. NOVEMBER 1858

PLATE 27. JULY 1861

a   b   c   d   e

PLATE 28. SEPTEMBER 1862

a   b   c   d   e

PLATE 29. NOVEMBER 1864

a   b   c   d   e   f

PLATE 30. APRIL 1864

PLATE 31. JUNE 186=

a   b   c   d   e

PLATE 32. JANUARY 1865

a   b   c   d   e   f

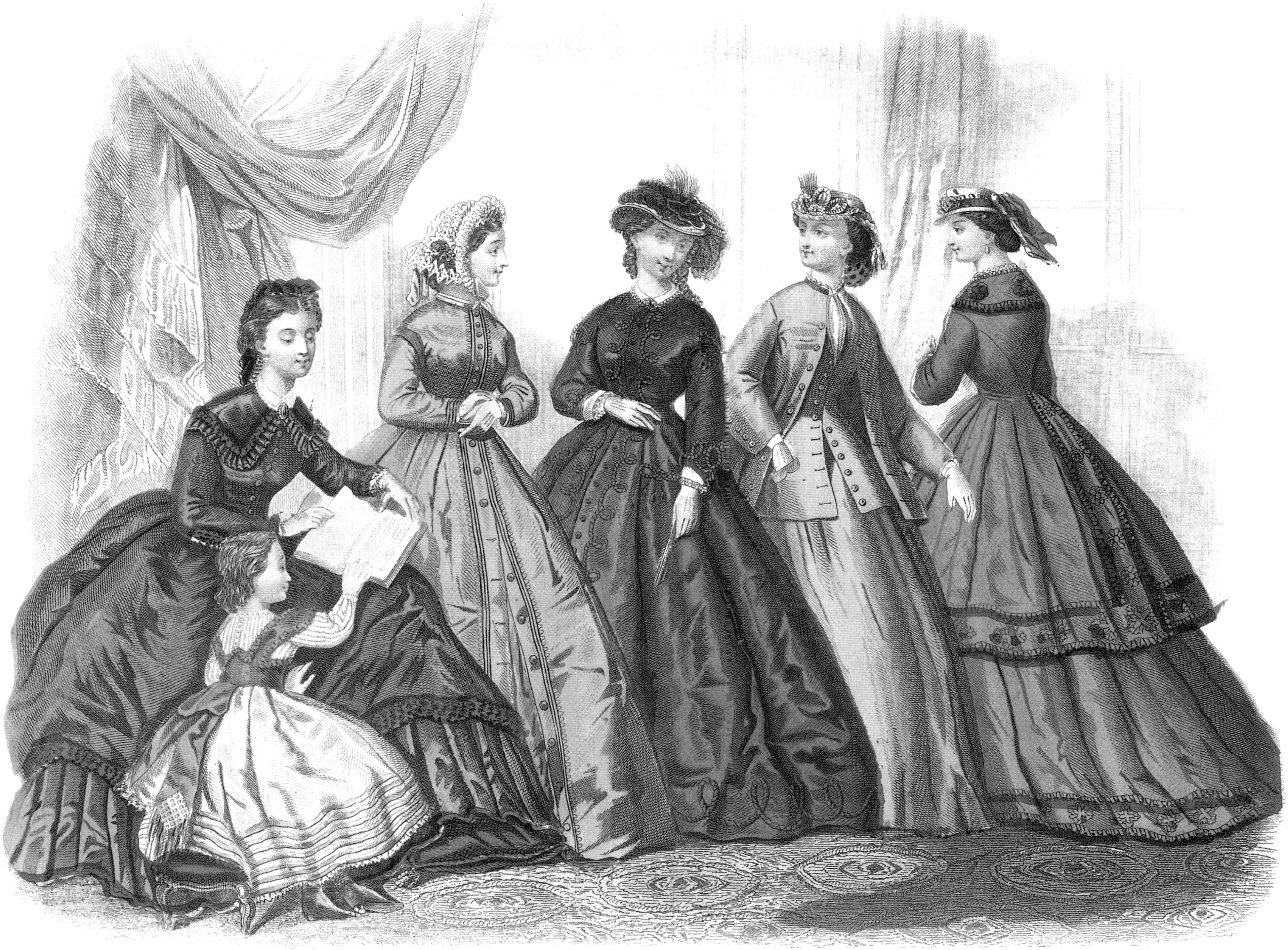

a *b* *c* *d* *e* *f*

Plate 33. April 1865

Plate 34. March 1865

a   b   c   d   e   f

PLATE 35. NOVEMBER 1865

a   b   c   d   e   f

PLATE 36. JUNE 1865

a   b   c   d   e

Plate 37. May 1865

a b c d e

PLATE 38. OCTOBER 1867

a b c d e f

PLATE 39. DECEMBER _367

a b c d e

PLATE 40. JANUARY 1869

a   b   c   d   e   f

PLATE 41. MARCH 1869

a   b   c   d   e   f

PLATE 42. MAY 1869

a   b   c   d   e   f

PLATE 43. OCTOBER 1869

a   b   c   d   e   f

PLATE 44. APRIL 1872

a   b   c   d   e   f

a   b   c   d   e   f

PLATE 45. JULY 1872

PLATE 46. NOVEMBER 1872

a   b   c   d   e   f

PLATE 47. FEBRUARY 1873

a   *b*   *c*   *d*   *e*   *f*

PLATE 48. MARCH 1873

a   *b*   *c*   *d*   *e*

PLATE 49. APRIL 1873

a   b   c   d   e   f

PLATE 51. MAY 1874

a   *b*   *c*   *d*   *e*

a b c d e f

PLATE 52. JULY 1874

PLATE 53. SEPTEMBER 1874

a   b   c   d   e   f

PLATE 54. OCTOBER 1874

a   b   c   d   e   f

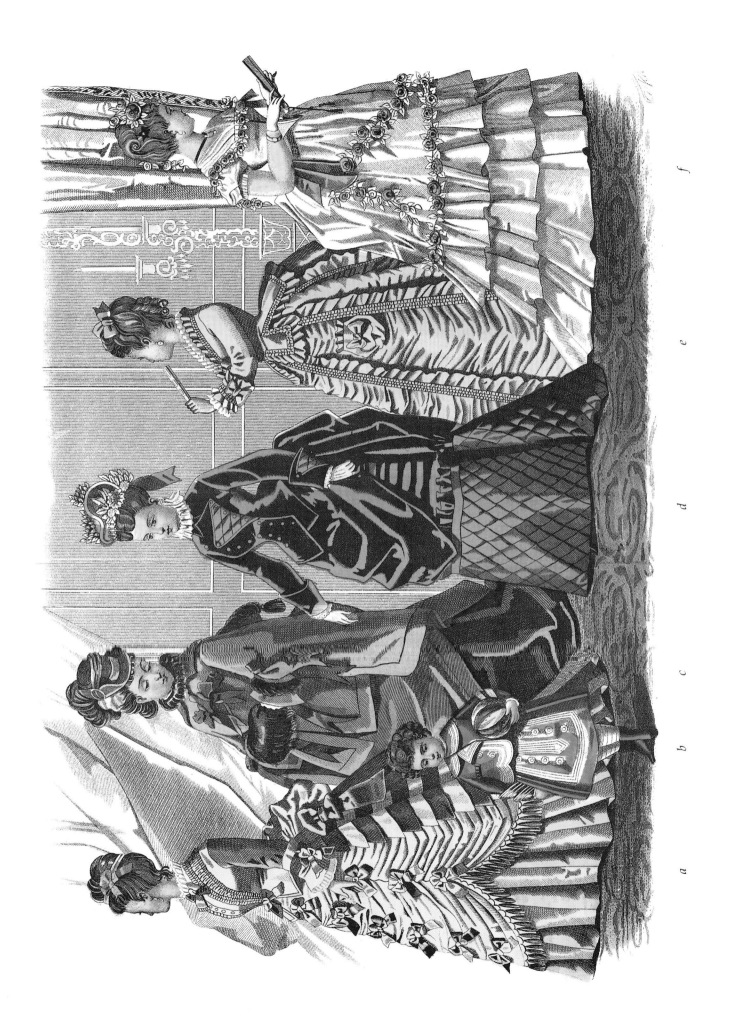

Plate 55. November 1874

a   b   c   d   e   f

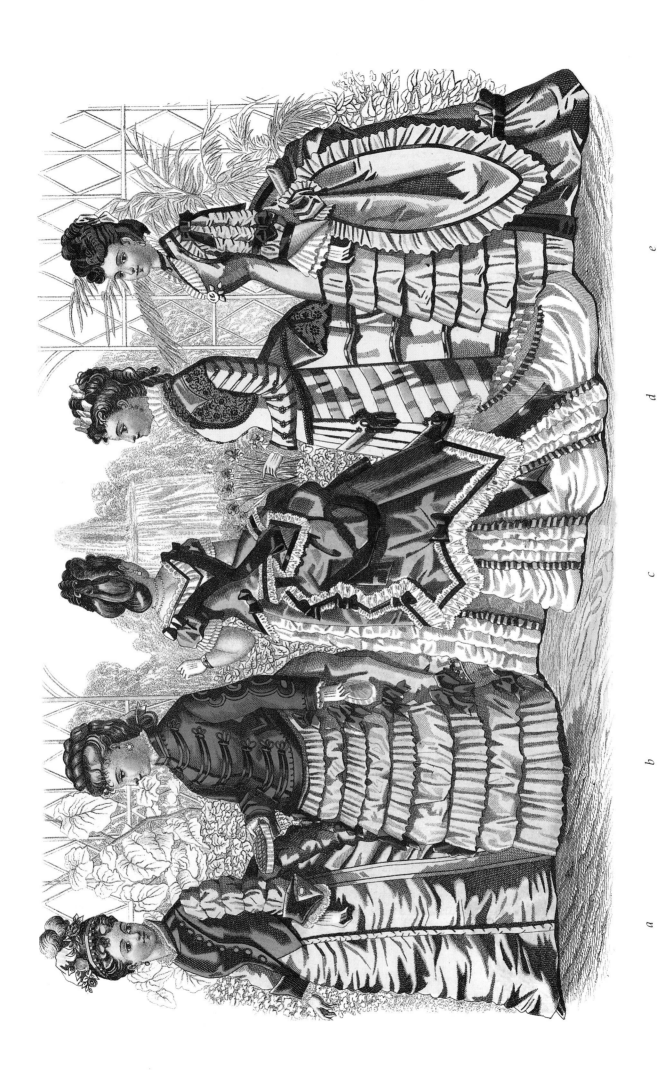

PLATE 56. MAY 1875

a   b   c   d   e

PLATE 61. MAY 1876

a   *b*   *c*   *d*   *e*   *f*

PLATE 62. JULY 1876

a b c d e

PLATE 63. AUGUST 1876

a   b   c   d   e

PLATE 64. OCTOBER 1876

a *b* *c* *d* *e*

PLATE 67. FEBRUARY 1877

a b c d e f

a   b   c   d   e   f

PLATE 68. MARCH 1877

PLATE 71. MARCH 1878

a b c d e

PLATE 72. APRIL 1878

a   b   c   d   e

PLATE 73. JULY 1878

a   b   c   d   e

PLATE 74. FEBRUARY 1879

a   b   c   d   e   f

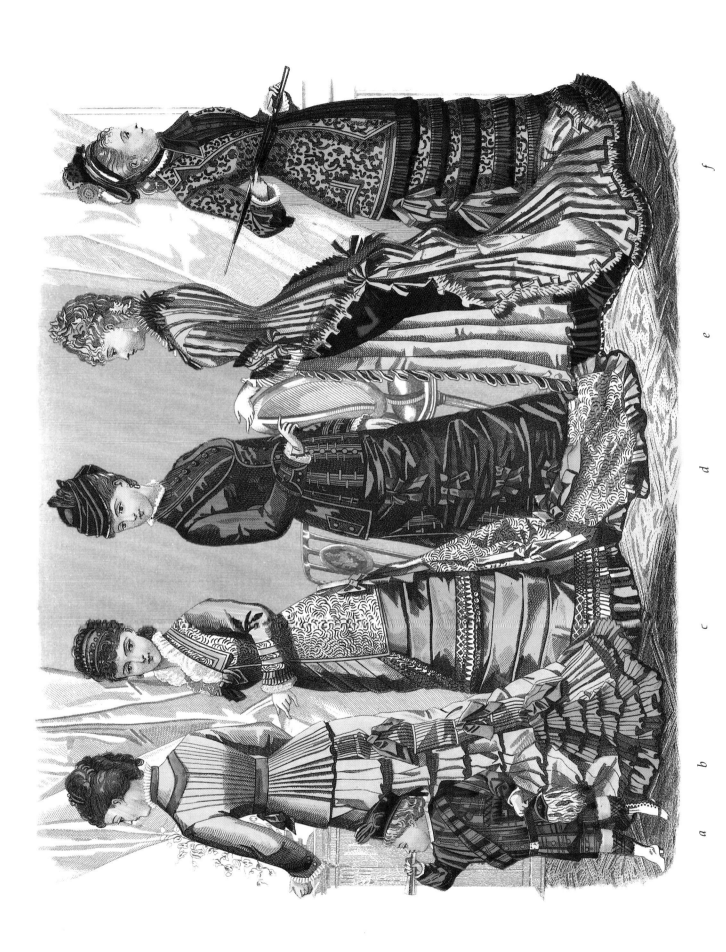

PLATE 75. MARCH 1879

a   b   c   d   e   f

PLATE 76. JUNE 1879

a   b   c   d   e   f

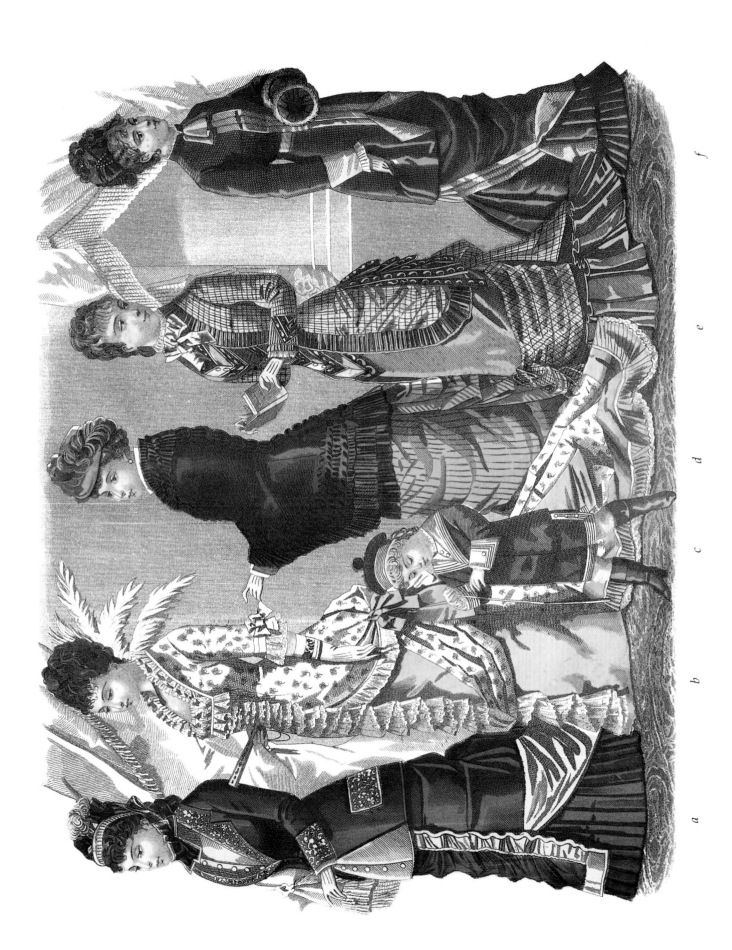

PLATE 78. OCTOBER 1880

a   b   c   d   e   f

PLATE 79. NOVEMBER 1880

a   b   c   d   e   f

PLATE 80. DECEMBER 1880

a *b* *c* *d* *e* *f*